Maria Wilson

The Christian Brothers

Their Origin and Work

Maria Wilson

The Christian Brothers
Their Origin and Work

ISBN/EAN: 9783744659628

Printed in Europe, USA, Canada, Australia, Japan

Cover: Foto ©Lupo / pixelio.de

More available books at **www.hansebooks.com**

THE
CHRISTIAN BROTHERS

THEIR ORIGIN AND WORK

WITH A SKETCH OF

THE LIFE OF THEIR FOUNDER

THE VENERABLE

JEAN BAPTISTE DE LA SALLE

BY

MRS. R. F. WILSON

"Come, ye children, and hearken unto me: I will teach you the fear of the Lord."—PSALM xxxiv. 11

LONDON
KEGAN PAUL, TRENCH & CO., 1, PATERNOSTER SQUARE
1883

PREFACE.

THE sketch here given of the life and character of the founder of the Christian Brothers is taken (much abridged) from the "Histoire du Venerable Jean Baptiste de la Salle, par Armand Ravelet," published in 1874. For the notes on the after history of the Institute I am indebted to the very interesting "Vie du Frère Philippe, par M. Poujoulat;" "Les Frères des Écoles Chrétiennes, par le General Baron Ambert;" "Les Frères des Écoles Chrétiennes pendant la guerre de 1870–1871, par J. d'Arsac;" and to other smaller books and pamphlets furnished to me by the kindness of M. l'Abbé Martin; as also to some of the publications of the Institute, sent to me by one of the Assistant-Superiors at Paris, to whom, as well as to the Abbé Martin, I return grateful thanks.

I cannot but acknowledge at the same time the great kindness and affability with which Monseigneur Langénieux, the Archbishop of Rheims, received unknown strangers, and in every way facilitated our inquiries; and the extreme courtesy and hearty goodwill with which M. l'Abbé Meinil, Chaplain of the Brothers at Rheims, devoted his time to our service, showing us all over the Pensionnat des Frères, and other points of interest in that city.

If these lines should ever meet his eye, I hope he will accept them as the expression of a very grateful remembrance of his kindness.

M. W.

Rownhams, Southampton,
August, 1883.

CONTENTS.

CHAPTER I.

Introductory 1

CHAPTER II.
1651-1678.

Birth and childhood of J. B. de la Salle—Early vocation to the Priesthood—Is made Canon of Rheims—Studies at Saint Sulpice—Loss of his parents—Return to Rheims—Ordination—Canon Roland bequeaths to him the care of an orphanage 12

CHAPTER III.
1678-1682.

Madame de Maillefer—Her conversion—She founds a school for boys at Rheims—A second is founded by another lady—De la Salle interests himself in the masters—Takes a house for them—Has them to dine with him—Takes them to live with him 24

CHAPTER IV.

Education in France during the Middle Ages—Encyclical of Charlemagne—Decay of education after his time—Canons of councils concerning it—Diocesan enactments—Appointment of schoolmasters—Inspection of schools—Funds—Endowments—School fees 43

CHAPTER V.

Difficulty of finding schoolmasters—Religious Communities for teaching girls—Failure of such attempts for boys—Letter of M. Bourdoise—Association for intercessory prayer on this behalf 54

CHAPTER VI.
1682-1686.

Growth of De la Salle's work—Discontent of the masters—He proposes to resign his stall—Is forbidden by his Director—Consults Père Barré—The Archbishop accepts his resignation—He distributes his fortune to the poor ... 64

CHAPTER VII.
1686-1688.

Development of the Community—Preparatory Rules—De la Salle's humility and obedience—Death of several Brothers—He resigns the Superiorship—Is compelled to resume it—Foundation of the little Noviciate—And of the training college for ordinary schoolmasters ... 77

CHAPTER VIII.
1688.

Peculiarities of educational arrangements in Paris—Rivalry between schoolmasters and writing-masters—Parish of Saint Sulpice—De la Salle is invited there—Results—False accusations—Is attacked by the schoolmasters—His illness—Death of Frère l'Heureux 92

CHAPTER IX.
1688-1694.

Decline of the Community at Rheims—Establishment at Vaugirard—Famine and sufferings—Perpetual vows—De la Salle tries again to divest himself of the Superiority, but is twice re-elected 108

CHAPTER X.

Final drawing up of the Rule—Constitution of the Society—Time-table—Spirit of mortification and poverty ... 121

CHAPTER XI.

The Manual for schoolmasters—Its comprehensive character—Directions about teaching—On good manners—Counsels and cautions to masters—Characteristics of a good master 134

CHAPTER XII.
1698-1703.

Increase of the Community—De la Salle hires a large house at Vaugirard—Enlarges his work—Takes charge of young Irish gentlemen from the court of James II.—His success with refractory youths—Sunday school in the parish of Saint Sulpice—Complaints of severity—The Archbishop appoints a new Superior—The Community refuse to receive him 143

CHAPTER XIII.
1703-1708.

Removal to the parish of Saint Paul—Attack of schoolmasters and writing-masters—Sentence against De la Salle confirmed by Parliament—Is ordered to leave Paris—Establishes the Institute at Rouen—The Bishops of Chartres and Alais ask for masters—Schools are established in all parts of France ... 162

CHAPTER XIV.

1705-1712.

Educational arrangements at Rouen—De la Salle is invited there—He moves his Community to Saint Yon—It becomes the mother house of the Institute—Famine and distress—Plots and troubles—De la Salle determines to withdraw from public view 176

CHAPTER XV.

1712-1714.

De la Salle visits the houses of his Community in the south of France—Is welcomed by all, especially at Marseilles—The Jansenists there first favour him—Then turn against him—He leaves Marseilles, and spends six months at Grenoble—Visits the Grande Chartreuse—Is recalled by the Brothers to Paris 188

CHAPTER XVI.

1714-1717.

Difficulties during De la Salle's absence—He returns to Paris—Goes to Saint Yon—Visit of M. Gense and M. de la Cocherie—De la Salle visits Calais and Boulogne—Returns to Saint Yon—Resigns—Election of Frère Barthelemy 198

CHAPTER XVII.

1717-1719.

De la Salle goes to Paris on business—Lodges at Saint Nicolas du Chardonnet—Purchase of Saint Yon—He returns there—His last illness and death 212

CHAPTER XVIII.

1720-1833.

Increase of the Institute—Dispersion during the Revolution—Restoration by Napoleon I.—Night schools—Letters of M. Guizot ... ... „ 222

Contents.

CHAPTER XIX.
1838.

Frère Philippe—His character and influence—Saint Nicolas—The Brothers take charge of convicts—Spread of the Institute in foreign lands **236**

CHAPTER XX.
1870, 1871.

The Franco-Prussian War—The Superior puts all the resources of the Institute at the command of the Government—The Brothers on the battlefields—The Commune—The Superior leaves Paris—The insurrection put down—Peace restored—The return of the Superior... ... ... **252**

CHAPTER XXI.
1871-1883.

The Brothers resume their work—Peace and progress—Superiority of their teaching—Causes: natural, supernatural—Opposition of the anti-clerical party—Laicization—Efforts of the Church party to supply religious education—How responded to—Words of Victor Hugo—Conclusion **266**

THE CHRISTIAN BROTHERS.

CHAPTER I.

INTRODUCTORY.

THE question of education in all its departments, from the highest to the lowest, but especially primary education for the children of the working classes, has of late years been brought prominently forward; it has largely occupied the minds of thoughtful men, and much time has been spent by the legislative assemblies of most European nations in enacting and amending codes for the regulation of it. We hear much of the duty of the State to educate its children, a duty which, if somewhat differently expressed, hardly any would be found to deny; for surely it is right that the State should provide for the education of those who have not means to procure it for themselves. But the claim put forward goes far beyond this; the talk is not so much of *duty* as of *right*, the right of the State to enforce an education, irrespective of parents, or of the Church.

Nowhere has this theory been carried so far, or acted upon with what appears to be such infatuated blindness and cruel injustice, as in France. France, that land of extremes, where everything seems to be carried to excess, and moderation to be impossible ; where good and evil alike appear in an intensified degree; amongst whose sons may be found examples of the most heroic saintliness as well as of the most fiendish wickedness ; France, which to use the words of a living writer, a son of her own,* "seems to exist for the purpose of trying every conceivable experiment in her own person in order that other countries may reap the fruit of her experience."

Everywhere, throughout Europe, as well as amongst ourselves, education by the State, independently of the Church, and tending towards the exclusion, sooner or later, of all religion, is one of the burning questions of the present day ; but it is in France alone that a member of the Senate, representing a strong party in the country, has been heard plainly to declare the object of such legislation to be "to rescue the children from the clutches of the Catholic Church, and in order to do

* M. l'Abbé Martin, Professor of History in the Catholic University.

so, to snatch them from the hands of their parents, lest they should be given up by them to the Priests."

These words, in fact, afford the only explanation of what has been going on since 1879 with regard to the Christian Brothers. Of all European nations, France has the singular advantage of possessing in her midst a body of men—numbering over eleven thousand—who, at no expense or trouble to the State, have been trained with special care for the work of education, and the end and object of whose lives is to educate free of all cost, the children of the poor; men in whom self-interest, ambition, the desire to advance themselves in the world, can have no place, for, once committed to this profession, they can never rise to anything higher; men who ask for no pay, no remuneration of any kind, beyond being provided with the barest necessaries of life; men whose scholars when allowed to compete with others, carry all before them, not only in examinations in elementary knowledge, but also in the higher branches of education—music, drawing, mathematics, geometry, mechanics, natural science, etc.; men who are trusted and beloved by the people of France, and who have given the most striking proof that could be given, of their patriotism and devotion to their country. Such are the men whom the powers that be at this present time in France would banish (if they could) from the country; out of whose hands they would take (if they could), at an enormous cost to the nation, the education of the people. And why? They are not priests; they are pledged never even to aspire to the priesthood; they are laymen, taken mostly from the ranks of the working classes; but they are, as their name declares, Christians; they are religious, and they teach religion in their schools; their lives, their garb, their whole bearing witnesses to their faith in Christ. This is their crime; for this they are expelled, thwarted, plundered, persecuted. Can the infatuated blindness of anti-Christian intolerance go farther?

From the language sometimes used by the advocates of secular education, it might be supposed that all care for primary instruction had originated with them; that up to their time the people had been left to grow up in ignorance; that they had been the first to put books into the hands of the children of the poor.

But history shows that long before the State dreamed of taking any concern in the matter, the Church had not only discussed it in her synods and councils, and enforced stringent rules to secure the attention of her ministers to it, but she had also opened schools, devised schemes of education, written books, drawn up rules, founded institutions, trained masters, and brought into active existence all the machinery of popular education, of which the secular party are disposed to claim the credit; indeed, it is a noteworthy fact that while the Church has thus been all along consistently upholding and working for the education of the people, it was the secularists of a hundred years ago who opposed it. It was one of the anti-clericals of the eighteenth century,* who, in an essay on national education, declared that by their labours in instructing the children of the working classes, the Christian Brothers were come to ruin everything (*pour achever de tout perdre*).

"They teach reading and writing to people who ought only to learn the use of a pencil, and how to handle a file or a plane, but who will not care to work any more . . . . . The good of society demands that the learning of the people should not go beyond their occupations. Amongst the working classes hardly any one need know how to read and write except those whose living depends on it."

And Voltaire, commenting on the essay which had been sent to him in manuscript, writes—

"I think all your views are sound. I am thankful that you propose to forbid working men to study. As an agriculturist myself, I beg that I may have labourers and not clerks; you might send me some of those 'Frères Ignorantins'† to drive my ploughs, or to draw them." (Letter of Feb. 28, 1763.)

---

* La Chalotais.
† "Frères Ignorantins." The derivation of this name is doubtful; it was not originally used as a term of reproach. Some say that from the chief establishment of the Christian Brothers being at

Contrast these supercilious words of Voltaire, who may fairly be taken as the representative in his own day of the anti-clerical and secularist spirit, with those of the Pope, Benedict XIII., when in giving his solemn sanction to the Institute of the Christian Brothers, he deplores—

"The scandals which spring from ignorance, the source of all evils, especially among those who, weighed down by poverty, or obliged to work for their living, are quite without learning,"

and no unprejudiced mind can fail to see on which side was the real desire for liberty, fraternity, and equality.

The professions of the secularists of the nineteenth century, are, it is true, very different in words; public opinion would not endure such sentiments now, and any one who should put them forth in words, in the present day, would be self-condemned; but is it possible to believe that their professions of zeal for the education of the poor are sincere, when we find them arbitrarily taking it out of the hands of those who by every test that can be impartially applied, are proved to be most efficient? How is such fierce antagonism to be accounted for against those who have produced the best results, at the smallest cost, their enemies themselves being judges?

Saint Yon, they got the name of Frères Yontains, and that it was gradually corrupted into Frères Ignorantins. Others suppose that the title was given to them because of the rule, which their founder strictly enforced, that none of them should learn Latin.

Introductory.

It has been said that "the reproach brought against their religious teaching is not serious," and that their real offence is their independence of the State, "that government officials cannot exercise much influence over them." But if so, why is the same animosity displayed, the same measures of expulsion adopted, towards the religious Sisters, who nurse the sick in hospitals?

We can understand the state of mind which desires to turn every schoolmaster into a political agent, but what object can there possibly be in government officials exercising influence over the sick and aged, the helpless and the dying poor?

What but the anti-Christian spirit which cannot abide that which speaks of faith in the unseen, could be the motive for depriving of all religious ministries and consolations, those who have no other hope, no other consolation in the world?*

Those who would banish, as far as in them lies, religion from the hospital, are the same who would banish the name of God from the school, and who, to carry out their purpose, not only tear down the crucifix from the walls, but choose the moment to perpetrate this outrage when the children are all assembled, that those young and innocent and wondering eyes may witness the insults thus

---

* Since these words were written, a further step has been taken in the same direction, by the suppression of all hospital chaplains in Paris.

offered to the image of their God and their Redeemer.

But who and what are the "Brothers" against whom so much bitterness has been shown, whom Voltaire would have harnessed to his ploughs, and out of whose hands a small but overbearing minority has tried to take the education of the children of the people in France? They are a very remarkable body of men; the special character of their devotion is that they have consecrated themselves to a life, in which, to quote the words of an eloquent French speaker* on the subject, they have—

"Neither the joys of family life, nor the consolations of the Priesthood; neither the lawful pride of hearth and home, nor that dignity which from the altar is conveyed to the Priest, and clothes him with a kind of majesty. In their poor and monotonous existence, wholly devoted to a toil as unremitting as it is inglorious, they meet with many trials, and are exposed to great ingratitude, but they are supported by two principles, which together form the motive power of their life, viz. the love of God, and the love of the people."

Amongst the numerous English travellers who, either for health or pleasure, make more or less lengthened residences abroad, there must be many whose interest in parochial work at home has led them to visit the schools in the places where they have been staying. To such the figures of the

* M. Chesnelong.

Frères Chrétiens are probably familiar, or used to be before the unhappy legislation of the last four years.

The perfect order and good management of their schools, the gentle quiet voices of the Brothers, never raised in loud or angry tones, the way in which all the proceedings of a school of perhaps a hundred boys are conducted almost without a word, by the use of the little wooden signal, at whose sharp though toneless sound every eye is raised, and fixed on the teacher, and every manœuvre of the school performed with ready precision, under its well understood word of command; these things must have struck those who have watched the conduct of schools by the Christian Brothers; but few if any are aware that all this excellent and effective system was the invention of their founder, the Venerable Jean Baptiste de la Salle.

In any survey of popular education in France, his figure must of necessity occupy a prominent place, and it is by the study of his life that we shall best arrive at a true understanding of the aim and object, as well as of the character and early history, of the Institute of the Christian Brothers. Before his time there were zealous workers, who did their best to carry out the injunctions and intention of the Church in the matter of education; but there was no unity of design in their work, and they lacked the power and efficiency which comes from united systematic action.

He was the first to gather round him a body of Christian Schoolmasters, and gradually to form them into a Religious Community, with a regular noviciate for their training and preparation, a Superior to guide and direct them, and homes to receive them when they could no longer carry on their work. He induced them to give up their names, their families, their property, in order to a more unreserved dedication of themselves to the care of the lambs of Christ's flock. Before putting such counsels before them, he put them in practice himself. He gave up a position of ease, comfort, wealth, and dignity, as Canon of Rheims, to become an humble schoolmaster, and the head of a numerous family which has since spread through the world.

He may be said to have been the first to reduce to a scientific system, elementary school teaching; and by making it a rule that none of his community should learn Latin, he prevented schools designed for the poor from being gradually transformed into colleges or higher class schools, whereby those for whose benefit they were founded would again be left without means of education.

To elementary day schools he added boarding schools for children without homes, or whom it was necessary to remove from their homes; reformatory schools for those who had fallen into crime; Sunday schools for those who were at work in the week; besides preparatory schools for masters who had no vocation to join his strictly religious community, the originals of our Training Colleges. In short, it may be said that from his hands came forth a complete machinery of primary education, perfect in all its departments, forestalling by nearly two hundred years our educational system of the present day.

And it was not to France alone that he gave schools. His system and the Brothers of his Institute have spread throughout the world. To him his country owes this honour—that Christian nations, far and near, have applied to her to learn how to educate the children of the poor, and to this end, have borrowed her books, her methods, and her masters.

Such was the man from whom sprang the now despised and persecuted order of the Christian Brothers, and whose story, involving, as it does, the early history of his Institute, we propose to tell. His gentle, and at the same time majestic, figure appears towards the end of the seventeenth century—an era full of great men, and brilliant with great successes, both of literature and of arms, but to whose lustre he in his humility and retirement contributed works as precious in the eyes of the Church as hose of Bossuet, victories more lasting than those of Louis XIV.

CHAPTER II.

BIRTH AND EARLY LIFE OF JEAN BAPTISTE DE LA SALLE.

1651-1678.

THE traveller who visits Rheims, and amid the modern buildings of the new town looks out for the far more interesting remains of the ancient city, may observe in the Rue de l'Arbalête No. 4, a large old house which bears, even in its present condition of evident decay, traces of former grandeur. A frieze, decorated with military trophies, and with a shield whose armorial bearings are defaced, runs round the house. Between two of the windows is a deeply carved stone niche, from which the statue has disappeared; on each side of the principal entrance is a half-length stone figure, life size—the one a bearded man, the other a woman. The tradition of the country is that these figures represent Adam and Eve, and were placed there by a certain Adam le Linier, a famous linen merchant of the fourteenth century. The Rue de l'Arbalête, then called Rue de la Chauvrerie, was the centre of commerce for the linen manufacture of Rheims, which at that time rivalled that of Flanders. Passing through the archway, which forms the principal or street entrance, the traveller will find a court, which, though now disfigured by workshops, must have formed a handsome quadrangle, with an inner façade and entrance, still in perfect preservation, and approached by a double flight of stone steps. In the right-hand corner of the court may be seen a graceful circular turret, containing a winding staircase, supported by buttresses and decorated with an elaborate frieze, similar to that on the street front. A tablet recently let into the wall records the fact that Jean Baptiste de la Salle was born in this house, and it is interesting to note the size, the richness of decoration, and the general character of the building, as showing plainly the worldly position to which he was born, and which he gave up to follow his vocation, just as the sight of the glorious cathedral, with its unrivalled exterior and its wealth of grand historical associations, not to speak of wealth of a more material kind, enables one better to realize the sacrifice which he must have made in resigning his stall and laying down all the dignity attaching to a member of so distinguished a chapter.

The family De la Salle was noble, and came

originally from Bearn. It was divided into several branches; that one which settled in Champagne had chiefly followed the profession of arms. One Menault de la Salle had been a distinguished officer in the army of Charles VIII., and had fought under the Chevalier Bayard. His grandson Lancelot settled at Rheims. He is described in the records of the town as an honourable burgess of Rheims, without any other title or description. He married Mademoiselle Barbe Coquebert, by whom he had three children—two sons, Simon and Louis, and a daughter Marie. After his father's death Louis, the second son, continued to live with his mother. In 1650 he married, and on the 30th of April, 1651, his first child was born, and baptized the same day by the name of Jean Baptiste. This infant was to be the future founder of the great educational order of the Christian Brothers.

From his earliest years the child showed signs of a strong devotional turn, which was fostered by the religious habits of the family. His grandfather, though a layman, was in the habit of reciting daily the Breviary Offices; he taught his little grandson to do the same, and the boy took such delight in them that he never gave up the custom, but continued to say them of his own free will, until he was bound to do so by his ordination. It was evident that his vocation was to the ecclesiastical life, and his parents do not appear to have made any opposition to it, although, as he was their eldest son, they might not unnaturally have desired that he should embrace a profession in which he might have handed on the family name and fortune to the next generation.

When he was about eight years old, Jean Baptiste was sent to the University of Rheims, where his diligence in study, docility, and conscientiousness won for him the esteem of his teachers, while all his companions loved him for his gentle, amiable disposition.

On the 11th of March, 1662, when not quite eleven, he received the tonsure in the Chapel of the Archiepiscopal Palace at Rheims, and by one of the strange customs (not to say abuses) of those days he was made Canon of the Cathedral five years later—before he was sixteen. An aged relative, who had been canon for fifty-three years, and felt that his death was near, resigned in his favour. Jean Baptiste was installed in his place on the 17th of January, 1667, and the old man died the following year. He was a good man, who had been Vicar-General, Archdeacon of Champagne, and Chancellor of the University, as well as Canon of the Cathedral, and he seems to have been fully persuaded that he was leaving his canonry to one of whom the Church of Rheims would be proud. The event proved that he was right, but it hardly justifies, in our eyes at least, such a manner of disposing of church preferment.

The Chapter of Rheims was one of the wealthiest and most illustrious in France. It numbered fifty-six canons, and sixty-one chaplains, appointed for the discharge of certain functions, for which provision was made by special foundations. At the end of the eighteenth century, thirty-one of its members had been Bishops, twenty had filled the Archiepiscopal See of Rheims, twenty-one had been Cardinals, and four had been raised to the Papal chair, and had heaped benefits on the body to which they had belonged. It was a strong step, even in those days, to make a youth of fifteen a member of such a body, but as Chancellor of the University, the old canon had had some years' acquaintance with young De la Salle, and he did not neglect to warn him of the responsibilities of the appointment. "My little cousin," he said, "remember that a Canon should be like a Carthusian, and spend his life in solitude and retirement." Jean Baptiste never forgot this counsel. From the first, he looked upon his preferment as a call to new duties; he was regular in all the offices of the Church, constant in private prayer, and, as before, diligent in study.

He set himself at once to prepare to receive minor orders. Cardinal Barberini was then Archbishop-designate of Rheims, but his appointment had not been completed, and the See was in fact vacant. The young canon, together with other candidates, was obliged to go to Cambrai, where he received minor orders, on the 17th of March, from the Bishop of Soissons.

Each onward step deepened his sense of the need of careful preparation, in order that he might worthily fill the place and office to which he had been called. As Canon, he was bound to study theology, that he might take his place among the eminent men into whose ranks he had been admitted. He therefore, at once, on his return from Cambrai, resumed his course at the University, where he took his degree as Master of Arts, with no small distinction, in 1669. Thence he went for more special theological training to the Seminary of Saint Sulpice, in Paris, which had been founded by M. Olier just about the time of his birth. He entered it on the 18th of October, 1670, and his name may still be seen in the register of admissions to the seminary: "J. Baptiste de la Salle, Acolyte et Chanoine de Reims." Several eminent divines were his fellow students, amongst them Francois de Fénelon, the future Archbishop of Cambrai, but he does not appear to have made his acquaintance; probably they were lodged in different parts of the college.

Little is recorded of him while at Saint Sulpice. The testimony of one of the masters is on record, to the blameless character of his life as a student:—

"He was from the first," writes M. Lechassier, "faithful in his observance of the rule, and exact in all the exercises of the community. Very soon he appeared to be more entirely withdrawn from the world, than he was when first he entered the Seminary. His conversation was always gentle and modest. He never seemed to offend anybody, or to draw down upon himself the smallest reproach."

This peaceful life, so well suited to his disposition, did not last long. Within a year after he entered the college he lost his mother, to his deep grief, and a few months later his father also was taken. They both died in middle age, leaving six younger children, to whom Jean Baptiste must henceforth fill, as far as was possible, the place of both father and mother. His father died on the 9th of April, 1672, and on the 19th of the same month, the young head of the house left Saint Sulpice, and returned to his home at Rheims, to take the charge of his younger brothers and sisters, so manifestly laid upon him by Providence.

This great change in his position raised in his mind a doubt, whether it were indeed the will of God that he should persevere in his intention of seeking admission to the Priesthood. He had as yet only received minor orders, and was not irrevocably bound, by any outward act, to the ecclesiastical condition. Was the long cherished purpose of his life to be looked upon as in itself binding him irrevocably? Did not the death of his parents release him from it? Were not other duties laid upon him, which he could better discharge by a life in the world? Was it not possible for him to work out his own salvation, in a secular life, and might there not be even greater merit in giving up his own long cherished desire for the sake of duties far less to his taste? These and many other questions rose up in his mind, and friends and relations were ready enough to urge them upon him.

Clearly it was a question not to be decided for himself, and it was well for the young man at this critical moment of his life, that he had a wise and holy guide to whom to refer his doubts.

Some time before he had chosen as his spiritual adviser M. Nicolas Roland, one of the Canons of the Cathedral, a man of singular piety and devotion, and of great experience. He had received into his house a number of young men who were preparing for the Priesthood; they lived with him, and he directed them in their studies, and was also the guide of their spiritual life. It does not appear that De la Salle had ever been one of his inmates, but he had for some time had the blessing of his spiritual guidance. Knowing him well, M. Roland had no doubt as to the reality of his vocation to the ministry of the Church, and his judgment, decidedly expressed, put an end to his perplexities. He determined at once to take the next step, and two months after his recall to Rheims, he went again to Cambrai, where, on the eve of Trinity Sunday, 1672, he was admitted to the sub-diaconate, thus committing himself irrevocably to the ecclesiastical life. He was then twenty-one.

After this he returned home, and spent six years in retirement. He resumed his studies, which had been interrupted by the death of his parents; he would fain have gone back to Saint Sulpice, but the charge of his brothers and sisters made this impossible; he therefore remained at Rheims, watching over them, and providing for their education, while he followed the Theological courses of the University, and took his degree in Divinity. All his spare time was given to prayer and works of mercy.

M. Roland noticed the growing fervour of the young ecclesiastic, and fearing that his position as Canon would not furnish scope for his zeal, but might rather tend to damp it, he advised him to seek a more active position in the ministry, and to exchange his stall for a cure of souls in the town. The incumbent of Saint Pierre de Rheims was well disposed to the change, indeed wished much for it. Young De la Salle consented at once to what was proposed to him as a means of doing good, but the exchange could not be made without the consent o the Archbishop of Rheims, who was then at Paris. Thither De la Salle went, in 1677, to receive deacon's orders, and to lay the plan before the Archbishop, and ask his permission to carry it into effect. This was refused; the Archbishop considered him too young to be entrusted with the cure of souls, and that he ought still to make the care of his brothers and sisters his chief concern. It was a charge to which his office as Canon was no hindrance, but which was hardly compatible with a conscientious discharge of the duties of a Parish Priest. So the young Canon retained his stall, and the old curé his parish. To the latter it was a great disappointment. De la Salle would have accepted either decision with equal submission, but in his own inner mind, he did not feel drawn to parochial work, and the judgment of his superior was therefore a relief to him.

Neither had he at this time any particular drawing towards that which eventually became the work of his life, viz. the care of schools and schoolmasters. His attention seems to have been first turned towards this branch of Church work by his friend Canon Roland. He had interested himself much about an orphanage for girls in the town of Rheims, which had fallen under very bad management; he reformed many abuses, put things on a better footing, and grafted on to the orphanage free schools for the little girls of the town. Being in a feeble state of health, and feeling that his death was not far off, he was most anxious that De la Salle should take his place in the care and supervision of these schools, and of a small community of religious women, who were in charge of them.

But his Ordination to the Priesthood was drawing near, and much of his time was spent in preparation for it. He was ordained in the Cathedral of Rheims, on Easter Eve, the 9th of April, 1678, and very soon after his ordination he lost his beloved friend and guide, M. Roland.

He had been taken ill on Holy Thursday, two days before the ordination, and died on the 27th of April, leaving De la Salle his executor, and commending very specially to his care, the community already mentioned, which bore the title of the Community of the Holy Child Jesus.

It was not without effort that the newly ordained priest took up the work thus bequeathed to him by his friend. His own disposition was rather to the contemplative than to the active life, and although he had willingly given his leisure time to the service of the community, he had never had any intention of taking upon himself the burden of its management. Nevertheless he applied himself bravely to the charge, as a debt which he owed to the memory of the good Canon Roland.

His first care was to obtain for the institution such legal recognition as was needful to secure its permanent existence. This was not an easy matter. M. Roland, the founder, had attempted it and failed; but De la Salle succeeded in interesting the Archbishop in the matter, so that he undertook to obtain the letters patent from the king, and himself bore the expense of their registration by Parliament. He also gave large contributions to the funds of the community, which he foresaw would be a valuable Seminary for Schoolmistresses.

Having seen the wishes of his departed friend so far accomplished, and thus discharged his own debt of gratitude towards him, De la Salle resumed his former habits, and returned to a life of retirement.

CHAPTER III.

THE VOCATION.

1678-1682.

THERE was at this time living at Rouen a certain Madame de Maillefer, who was a native of Rheims, but after her marriage had settled at Rouen, where her husband held a public office. She had been endowed with those gifts which are most full of peril to Christian souls, viz. birth, fortune, beauty, and wit; and she had not resisted their temptations, but had thrown herself without restraint into the torrent of the world's pleasures. No dish was too expensive for her table, no jewel too costly for the adornment of her person. Her one thought was to astonish the crowd of her admirers with some novelty in dress or fashion; she lay in bed till noon to preserve her complexion, her afternoons were spent in inventing some new arrangement of her toilet, and in trying the effect of her ideas on a figure made to imitate herself, and her evenings in displaying her dress in the world of fashion, of which she was the acknowledged queen. On Sundays she attended the mid-day Mass, not to pray, but to exhibit her dazzling costumes, and to outshine other ladies who might have had the pretension to be her rivals.

Such was the person whom it was the will of God to employ as His instrument, for sowing the first seed of the Christian schools.

One day a beggar knocked at her door; vanity and self-indulgence had hardened her heart, and he was harshly repulsed. But he was weary, sick, and utterly destitute, and the distress which could not move the mistress, touched the heart of her servants. The coachman received the poor man into the stables, and he died there in the night. What was to be done? His body must be buried, and Madame de Maillefer must be made aware of her servant's pious and charitable action.

He came to her and timidly confessed what he had done. She discharged him on the spot for having dared to disobey her, then she angrily threw him a sheet to serve as a shroud for this troublesome corpse which had so offensively intruded itself into her house. The interment took place: in the evening, as she was about to sit down to dinner, she saw folded up on her chair the sheet which she had given in the morning. At first she was angry, because she supposed that the funeral was not over.

This was a mistake, the poor man was buried; but it seemed that after death he would not accept of anything from one who in his life had refused him a morsel of bread, and a mysterious hand had brought back the sheet which her servants believed to have been buried in the grave along with the body which was wrapped in it.

This event produced a deep impression upon Madame de Maillefer. She saw in it the Hand of God, and it had such an effect upon her that by His grace she became one of those instances of sudden and complete conversion, which have occurred all along the Church's history, from the day when Saul of Tarsus was stopped on his way to Damascus.

Her resolution was taken: she determined to break with the world which had been her ruin, and to make the breach at once, by a startling stroke. The following Sunday she went to High Mass in her parish church, dressed in all her former magnificence, but wearing over her splendid robes the coarse and soiled linen apron of a servant. This was quite enough to alter her position in the opinion of her former acquaintance. She was immediately set down as an absurd devotee, and her friends forsook her. Her object was attained.

Her table was reformed; all luxury was banished from it. She lived by rule, and vanity had no place in her life; her days were spent in the churches, at the foot of the cross, or amongst the poor. Her former self-indulgence made her austerities seem the more incomprehensible, and she became an object of ridicule to those whose idol she had formerly been.

After her husband's death her way of life became still more severe, and for fifteen years the general opinion in Rouen was that she was mad. But in course of time people began to discover virtues hidden under her strange behaviour. It became known that the large fortune which she no longer spent upon herself, was given to the poor, and wisely devoted to good and useful works. And so, after having been taken for a fool, Madame de Maillefer came at last to be looked upon as a saint.

Amongst her other charities she had liberally assisted the Community of the Holy Child Jesus, in which she had been interested by M. Roland, when he had visited Rouen. She conceived a great desire that something of the same kind should be done for the education of boys, in her native town of Rheims, and she talked to Canon Roland about it; he entered heartily into her wishes, and plans for carrying them out were being discussed between them, when his death seemed for a time to put an end to her design, and obliged her to seek other help and counsel in the matter.

She engaged a devout layman, named Adrien Nyel, who had had much to do with poor schools and other charities at Rouen, and was a person of energy and good sense, to go to Rheims and there open a free school for little boys. She undertook to pay him a yearly income of a hundred crowns for his maintenance, and that of a boy of fourteen whom he was to take with him, and she gave him letters of introduction to her relative, M. de la Salle, who received him kindly, lodged him in his own house, and assisted him with advice how best to carry out the work.

After due consideration, and consultation with the clergy of the town, it was decided to open the school in the parish of Saint Maurice, where the curé, M. Dorigny, a good earnest man, had for some time past been anxiously turning in his mind the possibility of providing free schooling for the little boys of his parish. When he heard that not only the needful money was forthcoming, but also the man to start the school, his joy was extreme, and he accepted without hesitation the proposal that M. Nyel should open a school in his parish, which was accordingly done in the year 1679. This was the first beginning—the germ, it may be called—of the vast organization of the Ecoles Chrétiennes. De la Salle had been instrumental in starting it, and having seen it established, he supposed that his connection with it was at an end. But he was again mistaken; the work to which God's Providence had destined him still lay before him, and this was only a first step towards its accomplishment.

The good report of the new free school for boys in the parish of Saint Maurice, inspired another pious lady of Rheims with the desire to provide the same advantage for the parish of Saint James. She was rich and childless, and she wished to consecrate some of her worldly goods to charitable purposes, and especially to endow a school for little boys.

M. Nyel, whose whole heart was in the work, and whose one desire was to see schools established everywhere, heard of her intention, and immediately called upon her to confirm her in her purpose, and explain what steps she ought to take. He advised her to consult M. de la Salle, who had consented to be patron of the Saint Maurice school, and who would be sure to help her.

But De la Salle was by no means so eager in the business. He was not so anxious for the extension of the work as for its consolidation; however, as this good lady had expressed an earnest desire to see him, he consented to visit her. She spoke much of the good the school was doing to the poor of Saint Maurice's parish, and besought him to help her to provide the same for Saint James's.

"I must take advantage of this favourable opportunity," she said, "for it is now a long time since the wish was put into my heart, and it would make me very happy if I could see it accomplished before I die." For this purpose she offered a yearly payment of five hundred livres during her life, and a bequest of ten thousand in case of her death.

It was impossible to refuse her earnest request, coupled with such liberal offerings. She died, six weeks after, without having had the joy of seeing the accomplishment of her desire, but her engagement was scrupulously fulfilled by her executors, and Saint James's School was opened in September of the same year. M. Nyel placed another master in the first school, and himself took charge of the new one, which was soon as prosperous as the other.

Thus the work grew, by little and little, and De la Salle found himself almost unawares involved in the affair. There is extant his own simple account of his feelings about it:—

"It was," he wrote, "by the chance meeting with M. Nyel, and by hearing of the proposal made by that lady, that I was led to begin to interest myself about boys' schools. I had no thought of it before. It was not that the subject had not been suggested to me. Many of M. Roland's friends had tried to interest me about it, but it took no hold of my mind, and I had not the least intention of occupying myself with it. If I had ever thought that the care which out of pure charity I was taking of schoolmasters would have brought me to feel it a duty to live with them, I should have given it up at once; for as I naturally felt myself very much above those whom I was obliged to employ as schoolmasters, especially at first, the bare idea of being obliged to live with such persons would have been insupportable to me. In fact, it was a great trouble to me when first I took them into my house, and the dislike of it lasted for two years. It was apparently for this reason, that God, Who orders all things with wisdom and gentleness, and Who does not force the inclinations of men, when He willed to employ me entirely in the care of schools, wrought imperceptibly and during a long space of time, so that one engagement led to another in an unforeseen way."

M. Nyel was nominally the superior of this growing body of schoolmasters. He kept school and managed the children admirably, but he was not so successful in managing the masters. Being of a restless eager disposition, often travelling, continually taken up with some new work, he could not help these men to keep up the spirit of recollection, and the regularity of life needful, if their profession was to be what De la Salle aimed at, a truly religious vocation.

The latter was quite aware of M. Nyel's defects and did his best to make up for them. He could not but take an interest in the men, as they had been brought together and formed into a sort of little community, in great part by his instrumentality. There were now five masters attached to the two schools; they all lived with the Curé of Saint Maurice's, but his house was inconveniently small, and the funds provided for them hardly defrayed the expenses of their board and clothing. It came into De la Salle's mind to take a house, not far from his own, and to establish them there, where he could more easily visit them, and where, to save expense, their food might be sent to them from his own kitchen. He consulted M. Nyel about this plan, and as he heartily approved, a house was taken for eighteen months, as an experiment. Here, on Christmas day, 1679, the schoolmasters were installed.

As soon as they were settled in their new home, he drew up a rule of life, to guide them in the distribution of their time. He fixed the hour for rising and for going to bed, for devotion and for meals, and he used to look in several times a day to see that these rules were being observed.

Meantime he continued his theological studies in the University of Rheims. He passed all the examinations and took his degree as Doctor of Divinity in 1681, at the age of thirty. These advanced studies seemed to be rather carrying him away from that simple primary education to which his life was to be devoted, and he was still as far as ever from realizing the course upon which he was entering :—

"I never thought," he writes, "that the care which I was taking of schools and schoolmasters, was anything more than an external care, or that I should ever have more to do for them than to help to provide for their maintenance, and to see that they discharged the duties of their office with piety and diligence."

He did not know that it was to be the absorbing occupation of his life, that to which everything else was to be subordinate; and that his theological studies were preparing him to guide the infant Institution, of whose birth he was hardly yet conscious, to lead his followers safely through the perplexities of the times, and to guard them from theological errors.

Without knowing it himself M. de la Salle was gradually becoming attached to his little band of schoolmasters. Though their roughness repelled him, he was attracted by their hearty good will, and he looked upon them as men whose office it was to lead souls to Christ. As such, he felt the need of their being themselves conformed to the mind of Christ, and fashioned after His example; and to this end he laboured incessantly. But his other occupations did not allow of his devoting as much time to them as he felt they required. His duties in the Cathedral as Canon occupied a considerable part of his day, and the rest of his time was taken up with study, and social duties to his family and relations. He could only steal scraps of time for the schoolmasters.

It occurred to him, that if they came and dined with him every day, it would bring him more into contact with them, the expense would be the same as that of sending out their dinners, and, without interfering, except in this one point, with his usual habits, he would have opportunities for more frequent intercourse with them.

This plan he at once adopted—twice every day the schoolmasters gathered round his table, one of them reading during the meal. De la Salle chose the book, and took occasion from it to give them counsels as to the duties of their profession.

This growing intimacy with men of so humble a class, and the increasing proportion of time which he bestowed on them and their schools, did not altogether please his relations, and they remonstrated with him. They said the work was beneath him, and that he was letting himself be absorbed by it to the neglect of more important duties. Instead of spending his time with strangers they said he ought to devote himself to his younger brothers, who lived with him, and on whom he could not force the company of the schoolmasters.

To these remonstrances he made no answer. The good he was doing was manifest, and he did not feel that he ought to give it up; on the contrary, he was even then thinking seriously of taking the schoolmasters into his own house to live with him entirely, as he found the hours of meals all too short, and was more and more convinced of the influence which he might gain over them for good by being more constantly with them.

The objections of his friends, however, made him hesitate, and the step would perhaps have been longer delayed, if M. Nyel had not, just at that time, been called away from Rheims, to see about founding a school in the neighbouring town of Guise. He was only to be away for a week, but De la Salle could not bear to leave the young men, even for so short a time, without supervision, and he invited them to spend the days with him. Their rule required them to rise at five, and after their private prayers to attend the six o'clock Mass. When they left the church he made them come to his house, and all the time that they were not in their schools they spent with him, eating at the same table, and observing all their rules of devotion and study, till the hours of Evening Prayer, after which they went home to sleep.

This went on for eight days, at the end of which M. Nyel returned, but that week's experience had brought to De la Salle's knowledge much in the characters and habits of the young men which must be corrected, if their work was to be carried on in the earnestly religious spirit to which he was endeavouring to lead them.

M. Nyel, who had hitherto acted as their superior, was not, as has been said, altogether well fitted for the office; he himself was conscious of this, and when he saw the improvement which had taken place during the short time that they had been under M. de la Salle's direction, he entreated him to take charge of them entirely.

It was an anxious question, and one which required much consideration, whether to do so or not. The only way in which he felt that he could effectually guide and train them was by receiving them into his own house; and besides the objections of his family, the criticisms of his friends, and other obstacles, he could not conceal from himself that to do so would be to introduce a disturbing element into his daily life, which had hitherto been so tranquil and calm, and to take upon himself a charge which was sure to entail trouble, anxiety, and expense.

But it was necessary to come to a decision, for his lease of the Schoolmasters' Home had nearly expired, and he must either renew it or decide to make his own house their home.

In this perplexity he went to Paris to ask counsel of the Père Barré, who had himself for many years been labouring in the cause of education, especially that of girls. He had founded a Training College and Home for Schoolmistresses, where more than thirty lived together, and kept schools in various parishes of the city.

Père Barré had also interested himself about boys' schools, but, strange to say, without success; he seemed to have no power to control the masters, who led disorderly lives, and generally ended by giving up their work altogether.

De la Salle told him what had been done at Rheims, how almost unconsciously he had been drawn on to take part in the management of the schools and in the direction of the masters. He explained to him the present crisis, and the reasons which made him hesitate about carrying out the plan to which he felt drawn, and he asked his advice.

Père Barré was decided in his counsel. The story came to him as a kind of revelation of the will of God, and as an explanation why he had never been able to succeed in the religious training of schoolmasters. It seemed plain to him that De la Salle, and not himself, was the instrument chosen for the work, and in the strongest way he urged him to go on and carry into effect his plan of living with the young men, and making it the work of his life to train them and lead them up to his own high ideal of true Christian teachers.

His advice settled the question. De la Salle went back to Rheims with his mind made up; and on the festival of his patron saint, Saint John Baptist, the 24th of June, 1681, he received the whole company of schoolmasters into his house.

This put the finishing stroke to the indignation of his friends and the amazement of the world. Hitherto, however strange they may have thought his conduct, there was nothing that they could exactly find fault with. He had devoted his time and energies to a charitable work, as any good man might do; he had taken souls under his guidance, a duty to which he was specially bound by his priestly office; these things did not, however, turn him from other occupations, or wholly take up his time. It was a very different thing now that he was making it the main object of his life, and seemed to have no higher aim than to be the director of a company of schoolmasters. It was absurd, they said, for a man of his birth and position to choose the society of such men—for a learned Doctor of Divinity to make companions of those whose office was to teach poor children their a, b, c, and whose own learning was very little in advance of their scholars. It was a scandal and disgrace to see a Canon of the Cathedral descend to such a position.

His family were indignant; they seemed to themselves to share in his disgrace. They had looked to his advancement to the highest honours in the Church, for which he was fitted both by birth, talents, and character, and they saw him turning his back upon all these, to give himself wholly to a humble and thankless office.

De la Salle bore patiently with their upbraidings, but he was in no degree moved by them. What did it matter to him that the schoolmasters were men of humble birth, if they were the servants of God? That their manners were rude if their hearts were tender? That they had a humble position in the world, if they fulfilled a high vocation?

The grumblings of his relations had this effect,

that two of his brothers left the house, and ceased to live with him. The eldest brother, who was deeply attached to Jean Baptiste, would not leave him, but went on as before. The second went to live with a brother-in-law; the youngest, whose education was not finished, was taken away by his relations, and sent to school at Senlis.

This separation grieved De la Salle, but he could not altogether regret it; it left him more free. One after another old ties were being severed, in preparation for the final breach with all that is most valued and esteemed in the world. But a greater trial awaited him, and one which seemed to threaten the total failure of the work for the sake of which he had incurred so much obloquy, and made already so many sacrifices.

The young schoolmasters whom M. Nyel had gathered round him, and who, under his direction, had led a very free and uncontrolled life, could not bear the life of obedience to which they found they were now expected to submit. Many of them were without any real vocation. M. Nyel had selected them hastily, and without much discernment. When they found themselves in a house where everything was as much under rule as in a monastery, and where they were themselves treated as if they belonged to a religious order, whereas they had no idea of being anything more than ordinary schoolmasters, they very soon took a dislike to the whole thing, and went away. Some were dismissed, as being entirely unfit for their office, and incapable of becoming so; and thus it came to pass that in a short time the house was almost empty. Only two of the original company of masters remained.

This was a terrible blow to De la Salle. His work seemed at an end. After having endured the reproaches of his relations, the ridicule of his fellow canons, the unkind criticisms of strangers, he found himself, after all, without material for his work—face to face, as it were, with nothing.

In this, as in all his troubles and perplexities, he had recourse to prayer; and in the beginning of the new year, 1682, fresh candidates began to offer themselves. He had already drawn up the rule and order of the devotional exercises which, to this day, are followed in the houses of his community, so that the new comers could be under no mistake; they knew what they were undertaking, and the rules by which they would be bound. Those who came seemed indeed to have been sent by God in answer to His servant's prayer. They were pious and devoted men, with a talent for teaching, and dispositions which fitted them for Community life.

Thus cheered and encouraged De la Salle gave himself with renewed energy to the work which he had undertaken; he lived with the men, and never ceased his endeavours to bring them by degrees, more and more, not only under the external rule, but also into the interior spirit of the religious life.

Without authoritatively enforcing rules upon them, he brought them to feel the need of them, and to express a wish for them; then having got so far he drew up a few simple rules, and laid them before them, not as *his*, but as *their own* suggestion. He did not press for their adoption, but when once any rule had been approved and accepted amongst them, he took care that it was faithfully observed, and himself set the first example of strict obedience.

For about a year he carried on the work in his own home; but the house was not well suited for the purpose, and besides it was in a noisy situation, where the fuss and bustle of a crowded thoroughfare exposed the young men to endless distractions. He therefore looked out for a quieter abode, and found a house just suited to his purpose at the entrance of the Rue Neuve.*

This he hired, and thither he moved his community on the 24th of June, 1682. He continued to occupy this house as a tenant till the year 1700, when he and two other ecclesiastics bought it for 950 francs, to secure it to the community for a perpetual possession. In the revolution of 1792, this house was seized, the Brothers were driven

---

* Now called the Rue Gambetta, a change of name, which, to use the words of more than one of the inhabitants of Rheims, is "une bêtise, qui ne fait plaisir à personne."

out, and did not recover possession till in 1880 it was bought, together with some adjoining buildings, at a cost of 10,000 francs, contributed by the faithful; and on the 24th of June, the anniversary of the day when they first entered into possession, the premises were given back to the Brothers at Rheims. The house is now their Home, and a school of above 400 poor children of the town is held there.

In leaving his paternal home, Jean Baptiste de la Salle severed the last link with his past life. He took leave of the memories of his childhood, and the joyous recollections of his youth; he withdrew himself more and more from the world and from his friends, and stepped boldly forward towards an unknown future, guided only by the love of God.

CHAPTER IV.

EDUCATION IN FRANCE DURING THE MIDDLE AGES.

In order to understand what the work really was upon which De la Salle was entering, we must take a retrospective view of the state of education in France before his time; it will thus be more easy to perceive what the Church had already done, and what remained to be done; and it will be seen how far existing institutions presented facilities or obstructions to his designs.

If a complete history could ever be written of the educational institutions of any country, it would probably reach back to the foundation in that country of the Church herself. The earliest records of education in France which can be relied on, date from the reign of the Emperor Charlemagne, who in the year 787 wrote encyclical letters to all Bishops and Abbots in his dominions, requiring them to establish schools, where ecclesiastics might "apply themselves to the study of letters, in order to advance in their knowledge of the deep mysteries of the Holy Scriptures."*

The Emperor's commands were obeyed, and schools were opened everywhere, in which reading, writing, and arithmetic, spelling, singing, and the Psalter were taught. These schools were of different grades. There were first those held by the country clergy, in which they instructed gratuitously all the children of their parishes, and taught them the elements of faith and religion in the vulgar tongue. Next came the Diocesan schools, and those of the Religious Houses, where the education was more advanced, and was intended especially for young ecclesiastics, and for boys destined to the clerical profession. Lastly there was the Palace School, held in the Emperor's own palace, by learned men assembled from all parts of the empire, in whose labours he himself sometimes took part.

After Charlemagne, the prosperity of the higher schools declined. Louis le Debonnaire, himself well educated, and a friend to learning, tried to revive them, but the Norman invasions were beginning to desolate the empire, and well-nigh to destroy all remains of learning and civilization. Charles the Bald made some efforts to restore the ruined schools, but apparently he failed, as after

---

* Thomassin. Vetus et nova Eccl. disc.

his time no further trace of their existence is found in history. Some few probably survived in monasteries, or even in parishes, but from the ninth to the twelfth century, after the invasion of the Huns and the Normans, the greater number of schools were entirely destroyed, the art of writing ceased to be known by laymen, and was only practised by clerics and monks.

That the Church was not satisfied with this state of things appears from the fact, that the third Lateran Council, held in the year 1179, under Pope Alexander III., issued a decree to the effect that to every Cathedral Church should be attached a school, for the gratuitous instruction of clerics, and of poor scholars; that a sufficient benefice should be set apart to provide a suitable maintenance for the head of the school, and enable him to give school teaching, free of all charge, to those who desired to avail themselves of it.

The same rules were re-enacted by the fourth Lateran Council in 1215, under Pope Innocent III. They were acted upon, as far as troubled times allowed, and from that time schools appear to have revived, not only in towns, but also in the country. Their numbers increased considerably in the thirteenth century, and in the fourteenth we find Universities founded; the manufacture of paper was improved, it became cheaper and easier to procure, and the art of writing became very popular.

But it is difficult to arrive at any definite statistics as to the state of primary education in France during the Middle Ages. It appears to have varied much in different places, but on the whole to have been more generally diffused than is commonly supposed.

Thus in 1375, in the village of Saint Seine in the Diocese of Autun, there is record of the schoolmaster having engaged an assistant to whom he promises to allow all the fishes which the little children bring him in Lent.* Proofs are extant of the existence at the same period of schools in more than thirty places in the diocese of Langres, some of them being at that time, as they are to this day, quite little villages; and in fifty-three parishes there are records of foundations, either for providing a school house or for the maintenance of a master.

Schools must have been pretty generally established when Gerson, in his treatise on the Visitation of Dioceses, written about the year 1400, counsels Bishops to inquire carefully whether every parish has its school, and how the children are taught; and to provide one wherever there was none.

In the earlier part of the fifteenth and sixteenth centuries, popular education again declined. First the wars with England, and later on the sad religious struggles, brought ruin and destruction

* Etat de l'instruction primaire dans l'ancien Diocese d'Autun pendant les 17me et 18me Siecles, par M. A. de Charmasse.

over the face of the land. Where the church was burned or pulled down, the school was sure to suffer the same destruction. But in the latter half of the sixteenth century, the canons of the Council of Trent on this point seem to have been vigorously followed up by Provincial Councils and Diocesan Synods, and again decrees were made to the effect that there should be a school in every parish, and that in places where the people were too poor to maintain a master, a competent ecclesiastic should be charged with the instruction of the children.

The Council of Cambray, held in 1565, under the presidency of the Archbishop of that See, with the Bishops of Tournay, Arras, Saint Omer, and Namur, enacted rules concerning the parochial schools, in which we find the following:—

"Bishops will take care to keep up or to restore Christian schools, for the instruction of children in the elements of religion. Schoolmasters must be provided for all parishes. The boys and girls must be, as far as possible, taught separately. The masters shall only use books approved by the Bishop. The curates, chaplains, and schoolmasters, shall teach the Catechism to the children on Sundays and holy days after vespers.

"The Curates shall inform themselves every month of the progress made by the children, and shall take all possible care that they be taught the fear and love of the Lord from their earliest years.

"The Rural Deans shall inspect these parish schools every six months, or at least once a year, and shall report to the Ordinary how the instruction is carried on in each."

In 1676, the Bishop of Angers writes—

"Among all the cares which the responsibilities of the episcopal office lay upon us, there is none which we feel more deeply than the instruction of the children. We therefore charge all our clergy to give a portion of their time to this work, wherever a school has not been established. In parishes where there are several priests, the junior shall be held responsible for this duty, or some other examined and approved by the Bishop."

Similar quotations might be made from other episcopal utterances, as well as from the Acts of the Dioceses of Senez, Avranches, Arras, Besançon, Chalons, Chartres, Autun, Poitiers, and numberless others, showing how general was the attention of the Church to this branch of her work. In some Dioceses, as in Arras, there were, besides the day schools, Sunday schools for children who were obliged to work for their bread on week-days;* and these schools were very specially committed to the care and supervision of the parochial clergy.

The manner of appointing schoolmasters varied in different places. At first the right of nominating them seems to have been held to belong to the seigneurs, or landed proprietors, and the patronage was exercised by them. After a time they ceased to care for it, and it became usual for the parishioners to elect a master, who was then either presented directly to the Bishop or Archbishop for examination and approval, or else presented by

* Statuts synodaux d'Arras, 1584.

the Incumbent to the Rural Dean, who, after due inquiry into his learning, and religious and moral character, gave him a certificate, on receipt of which the Bishop or his Vicar-general granted him letters of institution. In some cases the parish clergy appointed the schoolmaster, and in no case could a master leave one parish to go to another without a certificate from the priest of the parish where he had served, of a good life and moral character.*

In the Diocese of Autun the schoolmaster was always chosen by the inhabitants jointly with the clergyman of the parish. No one was ever forced upon them. They made their agreement, generally in writing, promising him a certain salary, while he on his part undertook to keep school in that place for a certain number of years. Furnished with this paper, he went to the Bishop to receive institution, and if found capable, and of irreproachable life and character, the Bishop approved. If he was too poor to make the journey to the Bishop, he waited for the Archdeacon's visitation, and was instituted by him.

If a schoolmaster misbehaved, he was dismissed, but with certain formalities, which prove the careful and equitable diocesan administration of that period.

The Archdeacon, on his visitation tour, gathered

* Ordonnances synodaux de Meaux, 1669.

the inhabitants, by the tolling of a bell, to the church porch, and there, in the presence of the curate, they brought their complaints against the schoolmaster—of not properly teaching their children, using bad language, or any other misconduct. The Archdeacon then drew up a report, which was sent to the Bishop, who was the ultimate appeal in all such cases. His rights as supreme guardian of faith and morals were always reserved. It rested with him to take care that the people, and especially the children, under his charge were not misled by false teaching or bad example.

After their institution the schoolmasters were not left to themselves. It was customary to assemble them once or twice in the year, that their rules might be read over, explained, and enforced. In some Dioceses arrangements were made to give them an annual retreat of five days, in order to deepen the spiritual views of their office, and to strengthen in them the graces needful for its right discharge.

The supervision of the schools and the teachers was committed to the clergy. The curé was bound to visit the school frequently, to question the children, and to satisfy himself that they were well taught.

There seems, indeed, to have been a very thorough system of inspection established. First, that of the Parish Priest two or three times a week;

then that of the Rural Dean, once or twice in the year; and, lastly, that of the Bishop on his visitation tour. And the supervision was very close; it included both teachers and books. None were allowed but such as had been approved by the Bishop. Some Bishops had been at pains to compose books for the purpose and have them printed. Thus in 1570 a little book was published at Douai, under the title of " Christian Childhood " (" l'enfance du Chrétien "), written by the Bishop of Arras, and recommended by him to the schoolmasters of his Diocese.

The funds for maintaining these schools were frequently the fruit of the Christian charity of some private benefactor, who had also provided the school-house. And so it came to pass that many parishes possessed free endowed schools, which had cost the State nothing, and were no expense to the -inhabitants.

Where this was not the case, the endowments of the Church were drawn upon for the purpose; and the governors and trustees of Homes, Hospitals, and Lazar houses were exhorted to set apart some portion of the revenue of those institutions for the support of schools. The money so raised was supplemented by the "school fees." In the year 1685 the Bishop of Autun fixed the rate of payment in his Diocese at five sous, or twopence halfpenny, a month, for scholars who only learned to read; ten sous, or fivepence, a month, for those who learned reading and writing; and fifteen sous for those who were taught reading, writing, arithmetic, and Latin.

This was the rate for the towns. In country villages the payment was seldom more than one or two sous a month. Sometimes the schoolmaster's income was eked out by providing him with a lodging in the Presbytère, allowing him the burial fees, or granting him permission to make a *quête*, and collect what he could in the parish.

The villagers, too, had other ways of helping, such as gifts in kind from their gardens or poultry yards, or by agreeing to a voluntary rate, by which they secured a certain sum to the master.

It will be seen from this slight sketch of the provision made for education, that the instruction of children of the working classes was by no means so neglected in those earlier ages as we of the nineteenth century are apt to imagine. Not only was provision made for it, but constant exhortations were addressed to parents to remind them of the duty of sending their children regularly to school. Indeed, there are tokens of some approach to the compulsory education of our own times. Thus the decrees of the Synod of Arras, in 1584, enact that if in any place a difficulty is made about the building or maintenance of a school, recourse must be had to the

The Church's Care for Education. 53

Bishop, and even to the secular arm; and the same must be done, when necessary, to compel parents to send their children, both boys and girls, to school.

It cannot, in short, be denied that the Church had made education her special concern, and that there were found in France, throughout the length and breadth of the land, schools where the children of the poor were taught, much as in our own day, the three R's, together with the elements of the Christian faith. Without burdening the community with an education rate, heavy enough in our own case, but now still heavier in France, she had provided for the erection and support of numbers of schools. She had, moreover, drawn up rules for their management, so wise in theory and so successful in practice that they became the basis of educational legislation, both primary and advanced, in later times.

CHAPTER V.

DIFFICULTY OF FINDING MASTERS.

WE have seen what care was taken by the Church for the education of her children, and what abundant provision was made for it; and the question naturally arises, What more was there left for Jean Baptiste de la Salle to do?

But there was one thing which the Church had not succeeded in providing, and without which all her care, her rules and provisions were of no avail to secure a good education for her children, viz. trustworthy and efficient teachers. The clergy could not undertake the work themselves, notwithstanding the pressing recommendations of Provincial Councils and Diocesan Synods; it was impossible for the incumbent of even a small parish to shut himself up all day in his school, teaching children to read and write, and neglecting the services of the Church, the care of his parish, and his own studies and devotions. In large parishes there were, it is true, one or more curates, but the strictly clerical work of the parish was more considerable, and had to be shared amongst them.

All that could be done was to appoint one to have general oversight of the school, but not to take the part of actual schoolmaster. There were cases in which this was done, but they were rare, and it could not be considered a desirable arrangement.

It was necessary, therefore, to employ laymen; and as there was no institution or provision for training them, the clergy were obliged to take those who offered themselves. Sometimes it was a young fellow who had failed in his examination for holy orders, sometimes a stray lawyer *manqué* also in his profession, or it might be a peasant with a little more learning than his neighbours, who undertook to teach the rising generation the little he knew; or the parish fiddler, who would leave his school from time to time to play at weddings or village feasts.

It is evident that under these circumstances there could be no security as to the personal character of the teachers, and, in fact, complaints on this head are rife all through the seventeenth century. How bad they were may be gathered from the Acts of the Synod of the Diocese of Toul in 1686, in which the Bishop accuses the schoolmasters of his Diocese of being "gamesters, drunkards, profligates, ignorant, and brutal. They spend their time playing cards in the public houses, or playing the violin in places of amusement or village feasts. In the churches they are not suitably dressed, and instead of studying church music they sing during the service anything that comes into their heads."* Another Bishop states that in his Diocese, which was a small one, he had been obliged to dismiss twelve schoolmasters who corrupted the children committed to their care.

It was this deplorable state of things which gave rise, during the seventeenth and eighteenth centuries, to numerous religious orders of women, who made the instruction of the poor one principal part of their work. Some were wholly devoted to it. This sudden outburst of Christian charity was very remarkable. In France alone no less than fifty different foundations are on record within a period of one hundred and fifty years; and one remarkable feature of the movement was that in many cases these religious societies sprang from very humble beginnings, and arose out of a pressing need. How this was so in the case of the Sisters of Saint Vincent de Paul, who may be considered a sort of typical order for works of mercy, is fully recorded in the life of their founder, and hardly claims a place here, as their labours were

* Statuts Synodaux, 1686.

of all kinds and not primarily educational; but other instances may be given.

In the parish of Roye, in Picardy, the schoolmaster was dismissed for improper behaviour to one of the girls in his school. The charge of the school was at once undertaken by four young women, who, under the direction of the curé, lived together in a ruinous old house, where they kept school, and divided their time between prayer, the education of the poor, and manual labour. This modest beginning formed the nucleus of a religious order devoted to the education of poor girls, which soon spread all over Picardy under the title of Daughters of the Cross (Filles de la Croix), and to it was due the first institution for training schoolmistresses, established at Paris, by Mademoiselle de Villeneuve, and placed under the charge of these sisters.

Another instance of the same kind was at Puy, in Auvergne, where M. Tronson, one of the Saint Sulpice clergy, was curé, and sorely needing help in the care and religious instruction of young girls, applied to a devout lady of the place, Mdlle. Martel. She accepted the task, drew others into the same work, and they went from house to house, collecting the young women and girls whose principal occupation was then, as it is still, lace-making. They were persuaded to work together, uniting at the same time in prayer, and hymn singing, and without any interference with their ordinary duties, to follow a simple Christian rule of life.

This work, like that of the Filles de la Croix, grew to far more than had been originally thought of. The ladies found that they too needed help, and so trained village schoolmistresses to carry on their work, under the superintendence of the clergy. They were not bound by vows, or attached to any community, but they wore a distinctive dress, and followed a certain rule as to their practices of devotion. They became like guardian angels of the villages where they were stationed, teaching the children, watching over the young girls, nursing the sick, assisting the dying, and thus, hidden from the world, and wholly unknown even by any name, they fulfilled their sacred mission, and did their part towards preserving that faith and piety, which amid so much vice and infidelity is yet found in France, shining with a brighter and more striking light amid the darkness of the surrounding gloom.

But while every province of France saw some successful efforts made for the care and education of girls, the case was very different as regarded the boys. The need, indeed, was quite as great, and as deeply felt, but none of the attempts made to supply it had any lasting success or stability.

Gerard Groot, Canon first of Utrecht, and afterwards of Aix la Chapelle, had in the fourteenth century anticipated the devotion of De la Salle, by resigning all his preferment in order to give himself to this work, and had founded a community of clerics for the same objects; and at Rome Saint Joseph Calasanzio had done a great deal in the same direction, and also founded a community which did good service to the cause of popular education during his lifetime. But the work did not prosper after his death, which took place in 1648, at the age of 92. He, like Gerard Groot, made the mistake of having ecclesiastics instead of laymen as schoolmasters, and the consequence was that the instruction given in their schools gradually advanced from the simple standard required for the poorer classes, to Latin, grammar, and such studies as altogether changed the character of the schools.

The same mistake seems to have been made by all those who were moved to do something for popular education in France.

The most successful attempts were made by M. Demia, in the Diocese of Lyons. He did get together a band of lay teachers, and was soon beset by applications from the neighbouring Dioceses for schoolmasters, and many young men were sent to him to be trained, but he died in 1689 in the prime of life, and his work did not survive him.

Other attempts were made by good men, at Orleans, at Paris, at Beauvais, and at Rouen, but from one cause or other, none of them had any lasting success. Their failures, however, served as warnings to De la Salle, to avoid the mistakes into which they had fallen. He was thirty-eight at the time of M. Demia's death, and was already occupied with educational plans. He must have known the history of his endeavours in the same direction, and no doubt he profited by his experience.

It was the time of that wonderful revival of zeal and devotion, especially in the priestly life in France, in which Saint Vincent de Paul is, perhaps, the most prominent figure, but only one of a group of earnest, devoted, learned, and energetic men, such as are not often to be found in one country within the same half century. It was impossible that so important a work as popular instruction should be overlooked amongst the various reforms which were brought about by their means. In a letter to M. Olier, who, as the founder of Saint Sulpice, had done so much for the education of the clergy, M. Bourdoise, the friend and fellow worker of Saint Vincent de Paul, writes :—

"I could wish to see a school carried on in a truly supernatural spirit, in which, while the children learned to read and write, they might at the same time be taught and trained to be good sons of the Church. For it is a pity to see a large outlay of charitable funds spent in teaching them to read and write, without making them any better Christians; and yet this is what is most commonly done. In these days all children go to school, but there is nothing of a supernatural spirit in the schools to which they go, and one cannot wonder if there is but little trace of Christianity in their lives, since in order to have schools which should have this result, we must have masters who would undertake and carry on their work in the spirit of true Christians, and not merely as a means of gaining a livelihood.

"As to myself, I can say from the very bottom of my heart that I would willingly beg from door to door, to provide a living for a true schoolmaster, and, like S. Francis Xavier, I would ask from all the universities of the kingdom, men who were willing, not to go to India or Japan to preach to the heathen, but to make at least a beginning of this good work.

"It is easy enough to find among the clergy men fitted and ready for parochial work, whether as rectors or curates; but it is a very rare thing indeed to meet with persons of sufficient piety, and other necessary qualities to make them fit to keep a school, and discharge the duties of such a post worthily, who have at the same time sufficient means to make them independent of it as a profession, and who would be willing to undertake it, in entire submission to the clergy of the parish. So difficult is it to find such, that I am convinced that to labour to train such masters, would be a work more useful to the Church, and more praiseworthy, than to spend one's life in preaching, in the most renowned pulpits, in the most distinguished cities of the land.

"I believe that a priest of a truly saintly spirit might attain a higher sanctity in the office of a simple schoolmaster than in any other way. The best and greatest teachers, the most renowned Doctors of the Sorbonne, would not be too good for it. Because parish schools are poor, and have to do with the poor, they are thought to be of no consequence, and yet they are the only means to root out vice and establish virtue, and I defy any man, be he who he may, to find out a better. I believe that if Saint Paul or Saint Denys were now to return to France, they would choose the profession of schoolmaster before any other. But it would be needful that it should not be their only means of living, to the end that the people might esteem them the more highly, when they saw that they were neither dependent nor mercenary.

"For fifty-seven years," he went on to say, "I have been

well acquainted with agricultural labour, and during all that time, I never met with any farmer so ill-advised as to put the seed into his ground without having first well tilled and prepared it. Now it is in Christian schools that hearts are prepared to receive the seed of the Word of God when preached."

So full was M. Bourdoise of this thought, that he became the founder of an association for intercessory prayer, that Almighty God would be pleased to grant to France the blessing of Christian teachers for the poor.

He was at this time residing at Liancourt, where many ecclesiastics and members of religious orders, who had been driven by the civil war from Paris, were also staying. Seventy of these, amongst them many members of the Community of Saint Sulpice, entered into this association. All the associates were bound to pray without ceasing that the hearts of the Bishops and heads of the Church might be stirred with a great zeal for Christian education, especially for the children of the poor, and not only to pray, but themselves to labour in the same cause, and use all the means in their power to promote it. M. Bourdoise himself was most zealous in the fulfilment of these obligations. He wrote, he preached, he held conferences with his accustomed earnestness. One day when he had preached on the subject in the Church of Gentilly, his fervent words had such an effect that no less than eighty persons applied to be allowed to join the association.

This movement began on the 15th of March, 1649; two years later Jean Baptiste de la Salle was born. Amongst all the providential dealings of Almighty God with His Church, it would be difficult to mention a more manifest answer to intercessory prayer than this.

CHAPTER VI.

THE SACRIFICE.

1682–1686.

THE fame of the Rheims schoolmasters soon spread, and applications came to M. de la Salle from various places in the neighbourhood for masters. It was not without reluctance that he entertained them; he was not at all anxious for the rapid spread of the work, he rather desired to see a solid foundation laid in a small and humble way. But his friend M. Nyel was always ready and eager to enter upon new fields of work, and moreover applications were often made with such pressing earnestness that they could hardly be refused. Thus his community began to assume proportions which he had not contemplated, and with its growth it took up much more of his time. Whatever he undertook he did thoroughly and with his might, and finding that the incessant calls upon him were hardly compatible with the discharge of his duties as Canon of the Cathedral, he began to entertain the thought of giving up his stall. This was not a step to be taken hastily, but the more he considered, the stronger the reasons seemed to be in favour of it; and while he still doubted a fresh motive arose, which had even more weight with him than the question of time. The men began to show signs of discouragement and dissatisfaction. They did not complain of their present condition, but they were uneasy about the future. What would become of them when they were old and infirm? They would have spent their time of strength in unpaid toil, and must end their days in poverty and destitution. After a life of labour and privation, nothing but misery awaited them.

In vain their Superior tried to cheer and encourage them by reminding them that God never forsakes those who trust in Him; that He clothes the lilies of the field, and feeds the birds of the air. These words had no effect, and for this reason, that the men felt that M. de la Salle's condition was unlike theirs. It was very easy for him, they said, to have cheerful trust for the future; he would want for nothing; he had a canonry as well as a good private fortune to fall back upon—poverty could not reach him—the failure of the schools would not signify to him. But they were poor men, without any income and without a trade, what would become of them?

These remarks turned the scale, and decided the

question. De la Salle saw that if he hoped for success in his foundation it could only be by himself sharing the lot of his followers, in poverty and absolute dependence upon God. This could not be so long as he retained his canonry—the two positions were incompatible, and he must choose between them. One was a lucrative, comfortable and honourable office, for which, if he should make a vacancy, a hundred competitors would at once present themselves. The other was an humble and obscure profession, uncertain of success, promising nothing but toil and labour, without honour and without profit, and which no one was desirous of embracing.

This was the one he chose, and he resolved at once to send in his resignation.

But first he made known his resolution to his director, who strongly opposed it. He felt that an ecclesiastical career of so much promise ought not to be thrown up without grave reasons, that this determination might be the result of a hasty impulse, and that in any case it ought to be decidedly opposed, in order to test its steadfastness. If it was indeed the voice of God which called him to the sacrifice, it would triumph at last over all opposition, but for the present, he would not allow the force of the reasons which De la Salle alleged, he blamed his purpose, and charged him to think no more of it.

De la Salle submitted humbly, and obeyed his director as far as lay in his power, but he could not dismiss the subject from his thoughts, and the reasons which had decided him kept recurring constantly to his mind, with more and more force. The days were not long enough for all he had to do, and he could not prevent the men from comparing, with a kind of bitterness, the comfortable security of his position with the precariousness of their own.

After some months had passed, he made another attempt to gain the consent of his director to his plan, and was again told to wait. He waited, but he felt that in so grave a matter it was well to seek further advice, and he therefore went to Paris to consult the Père Barré. His judgment was different; he entirely approved of the design, indeed would have recommended even a further step in the path of holy poverty, by a complete renunciation of all worldly goods.

"The foxes," he said, "have holes, and the birds of the air have nests, but the Son of Man hath not where to lay His head. The foxes are the children of this world, who bury themselves in earthly things; the birds of the air are members of religious orders, who have each their cell as a resting-place. But those whose vocation is to teach the poor, after the pattern of Jesus Christ, should have no other portion in this world than that of the Son of Man."

These words made a deep impression on De la Salle; he believed that he heard in them the voice of God. When he repeated them to his director, he too was convinced, and gave his full sanction to the proposal.

Notwithstanding the great pains which he had taken to keep his project secret, a whisper of it got about, and caused immense excitement in the town. Surprise soon gave place to indignation, and there was a sort of conspiracy all round him to prevent him from carrying out his purpose. His relations, his friends, his fellow canons, his superiors, all united to dissuade him. No arguments were spared to shake his resolution. He was giving up sacred duties conferred upon him by the Church for a work full of risk, the success of which was very doubtful. Had he not formerly believed that it was a true vocation which had called him to be Canon? Did he think he could no longer please God in that estate? Was perfection only to be reached in singularity, and was there not really a secret pride at the bottom of it? He sought distinction as the founder of a religious order; he wanted to attract attention by his peculiar habit! Holier men than he had been led away by such temptations as these.

Such words of warning could not be disregarded by so humble a spirit as De la Salle's, and the unanimous opposition of all whom he loved, amongst whom he lived, and whom he was accustomed to obey, made him hesitate, and he had to pass through a time of severe struggle and perplexity. But in silence and retirement he sought to examine as in the presence of God the inmost depths of his own heart, and to test the purity of his motives; he weighed once more the reasons which had decided him against those now brought up to dissuade him, and the result was that he came out of this sore inward strife more entirely fixed in his purpose, and resolved to put it into execution without further delay.

It was the month of July, 1683. The Archbishop of Rheims was at Paris, and thither De la Salle went to tender to him his resignation; but he did not see him. The Archbishop was already on his way back to Rheims. As soon as he could get back, De la Salle presented himself at the Archbishop's residence; he was not admitted. Powerful influence had been used to persuade the Archbishop not to accept his resignation, and he, feeling that if asked he could not withhold his consent, refused to see him.

De la Salle was not moved from his purpose by these difficulties. He went to M. Philbert, one of the superiors of the seminary at Rheims, who had much influence with the Archbishop. He told him of his plan, and had his full approval. Then next he sought help where he knew it would not fail him; he went to the cathedral, and prostrate before the altar, he spent several hours in fervent prayer, beseeching Almighty God to guide and strengthen him, and to accomplish in him all His holy will. When at last he rose and left the church, he went straight to the palace, and was at once admitted. The Archbishop asked him whether in so grave a matter he had taken counsel with others. De la Salle replied that he had consulted M. Philbert. The Archbishop sent for him immediately, and he of course confirmed what De la Salle had said, adding that in his opinion he ought to be allowed to give his canonry to his brother. "He may give it to whoever he pleases," answered the Archbishop, "I accept his resignation;" and that same evening the archiepiscopal signature was affixed to the deed of resignation.

It was not without much and sincere regret that the Archbishop gave his consent, and he expressed his sorrow to many persons, but in his charity he said nothing of it to De la Salle himself, who was thus spared all argument and discussion. The obstacle which he feared might prove insuperable was removed, and the way made easy for his act of sacrifice. His joy was great, and as soon as he got home he assembled the community that they might all together sing a Te Deum in thanksgiving. Like the great Saint Bruno, who had also been a Canon of Rheims, and had given up his office there for a higher life, the venerable De la Salle was now free to follow the call of God, wherever it might lead him.

The brother, whom according to the customs of the Chapter it was proposed that he should nominate to his stall, was Louis, the one who had remained with him when the rest of his family had deserted him, and to whom he was tenderly attached. By bestowing his canonry on him he would have discharged a debt of gratitude for his faithful affection, and made provision for his maintenance. It would have been a gratification to him thus to requite his brother's love; but for that very reason he would not do it. He desired to make his sacrifice complete, and felt that it could not be so if the position and emoluments which he gave up remained in his family. When he sent in his deed of resignation, it was found that he had nominated as his successor one of the humblest and most devoted parish priests of the town, and the last person in the world who would have dreamed of being promoted to such a dignity.

This step, as might be expected, opened once more the floodgates of complaint and remonstrance. Every one had something to say about it. The Chapter, who were not at all reconciled to his retirement, wished at least to see his place filled by some one of as good birth and position. His relations treated it as an injustice that the income of his stall should not remain in the family, and they felt it a personal outrage that the young Abbé Louis de la Salle should be excluded from a place of wealth and honour by the act of his own brother. To his friends it seemed the act of a madman thus to throw away all that is generally most eagerly desired, and they said of him, as of his Master before him, "He is beside himself."

The Archbishop himself was not proof against these feelings. Great pressure was put upon him to induce him to withdraw his consent to the resignation. The Chapter wrote to him, all sorts of people got about him; he began to waver. Without withdrawing the permission which he had given to De la Salle, he made another attempt to induce him to give up his purpose through his Grand Vicar, M. Callon, who was also Superior of the Seminary at Rheims. The latter brought all his skill and eloquence to bear on the cause which he had undertaken, but so far from succeeding, he was himself convinced by the reasons De la Salle alleged in support of the course he had adopted, and the Grand Vicar ended the conversation with these words: "God forbid that I should recommend you to do what the world desires of you. Go on and do what the Spirit of God has suggested to you. This advice is the very contrary of what I came to give you, but it is right, and the only counsel that you must follow."

This unexpected assent made the good man very happy, and when the Archbishop was informed of the result of his Grand Vicar's mission he no longer hesitated. All formalities were concluded, and the new canon was installed on the 16th of August, 1683.

The loss of the emolument did not reduce De la Salle to poverty. He had still a private fortune of forty thousand livres, a considerable sum in those times, and he was determined not to live in wealth while he was counselling others to choose poverty. Since he had begun to break with the world by resigning his position and separating from his family, he resolved to complete the sacrifice by giving up his private fortune also.

Always prudent and deliberate, never impetuous, he would do nothing hastily, and as usual he began by consulting his director. His remarkable course so far, had prepared his spiritual guide to recognize in him a divine vocation to a life far above that of ordinary Christians, and though he could not but marvel at this last proposed act of faith, he did not oppose it, only counselled delay, and fuller consideration. To this De la Salle submitted with a humble docility. "I will not divest myself of my fortune if you are not willing that I should do so," he said, "I will only do so, as far and in such measure as you approve; and if you desire me to retain any portion of it, if it were but five sous, I will keep them."

A year passed thus. At the end of that time his director was satisfied and no longer checked him in his purpose, but gave him leave to do what he would with his fortune.

But now a great temptation assailed him, or what he looked upon as such. Since he was about to give his fortune to the poor, why should he not give it to those poor schoolmasters, who were really hindered in their vocation by their poverty? why not devote his money to the founding of Christian schools? There seemed much to be said in favour of such a disposition of his property, but an inward voice told him that it was better for the success of his work that it should have no foundation but that of evangelical poverty. His best adviser, the Père Barré, was of this mind. He had a great objection to all endowments, and thought that the sense of security which they gave tended to dry up the springs of grace in the soul. Particularly in the case of religious orders, he feared that the spirit of entire dependence on Providence, and perfect submission to the will of their superiors would be injured by it. Where there was an assured income, there would infallibly be applications from persons destitute of means of living, who would seek admission into the order simply for the sake of a livelihood. Motives could not always be detected, and thus the whole community would be lowered in tone.

"It would be much better," he said, "that the schools should only last a few years, retaining to the last their zeal and fervour, than that they should go on longer, by means of endowment, in a spirit of laxity and carelessness." "If you found, you will founder," was a favourite maxim of his.

This advice agreed exactly with the drawings of De la Salle's own heart. It was what he wished to do—if only he could be sure that it was right; but he knew that there were various ways of serving God, and that it did not follow that what was best for one institution, must needs be best for another. In his perplexity he sought for Divine guidance by earnest prayer. Very child-like and simple is the form of prayer which he is said to have used.

"My God, I do not know whether to endow or not. It is not for me to found communities, or to know how they should be founded. It is for Thee, O my God. Thou knowest how and canst do it in the way which is pleasing to Thee. If Thou foundest them, they will be well founded. If Thou foundest them not, they will be without foundation. I beseech Thee, my God, make me know Thy will."

His final determination was to give all he had to the poor, and his charity found abundant scope at once, for the year 1684 was a time of dearth; famine prevailed throughout all Champagne, and the poor of Rheims suffered terribly. De la Salle used to assemble the famishing people, and after a short instruction he distributed food to them. In every one of the starving crowd he saw the Lord

Jesus suffering according to His own word—" I was an hungered and ye fed Me." So vividly did he realize to Whom he was ministering, that he offered the food to each upon his knees, with the same reverence and holy joy that he would have felt in waiting upon our Lord Jesus Christ Himself.

This distribution of food went on for about two years; when all was spent, and De la Salle was become himself one of Christ's poor, he had occasion to go to the town of Rethel to confer with the Duc de Mazarin about the establishment of a Training School for Village Schoolmasters. Having nothing wherewith to pay for a conveyance he made the journey on foot, and begged his bread as he went along. An old woman gave him grudgingly a piece of black bread, he received it thankfully, and ate it with joy, for he felt that he was now indeed a poor man. He was at this time thirty-three years of age.

CHAPTER VII.

DEVELOPEMENT OF THE WORK.

1686–1688.

FOUR years had passed from the time that De la Salle first entertained the thought of making the care of schools and school teachers the work of his life, before the preparatory measures, recorded in the last chapter, were all finally concluded.

During this time his Institute had been gradually taking shape, and assuming more of the form and character into which he desired to mould it. His own singleness of purpose, earnest devotion, and saintliness of life, could not but tell on the characters of those who associated with him. While he set before them high aims and counsels of perfection, he made his own sanctification his first care. By severe mortification and daily discipline he was ever seeking "to keep under his body, and bring it into subjection;" born and brought up in wealth, and luxury, and having always weak health, he had been accustomed to delicate and well cooked dishes, and the coarse food, which as a poor man, he would share with his poor brothers, was a terrible trial to him. For a long time not only his palate but his stomach rejected it, and it was only by indomitable determination, and almost incredible efforts, that he overcame his repugnance. He conquered it at last by sheer starvation. He went without food till the cravings of hunger were so great that nature accepted thankfully any kind of nourishment.

But it was chiefly by constant fervent prayer that his soul grew in saintliness. He literally fulfilled the precept "pray without ceasing." He prayed by day and by night—his life was one incessant communion with God. He would fain have avoided even the interruption caused by sleep, and he grudged every moment given to it, because it shortened his time of prayer. He slept on the ground, or sometimes in his chair, and was the first to rise at the sound of the morning bell. While at Rheims he regularly spent Friday night in the Church of Saint Rémi; he made the Sacristan lock him in, and there poured out his soul in prayer for help, and guidance, and success in his work.

A spirit so ardent could not fail to influence and attract others. Students, or rather postulants, of various classes flocked to his house. Some were working men, others were of gentle birth, young men who gave up their secular studies, and professions in the world, and chose rather to learn, under his guidance, how to work out their own salvation, in the lowly office of poor schoolmasters. The house which he had hired in the Rue Neuve became too small for the growing community; he was obliged to take another in the same street, and he felt that the time was now come when the Institute should be provided with a Rule. He was far too wise as well as too humble to take upon himself to draw it up. In framing the law which was to govern and mould the community in years to come, he desired, first, the guidance of the Holy Ghost; next, the hearty consent and concurrence of the brotherhood; and lastly, the test of experience. He would not decide upon any rules till they had been tried, and found to work well.

He began by assembling the brothers for a retreat which lasted from the Eve of Ascension to Trinity Sunday, after which the twelve elder members of the body discussed the several points of the Rule with him. Each of them expressed his views freely and without restraint; the Superior listened patiently to all, and explained where he thought there was a mistake, but did not enforce anything of his own mind that was not cordially accepted by the rest. After all nothing was then done that amounted to a Rule, properly so-called. It was necessary to come to some sort of agreement on points affecting their common life, such as food, dress, employment of time, the name they should bear, etc. The material for the Rule would thus be prepared, but it was agreed that the final drawing up of it should be for the present deferred.

The first point discussed was the food. It was to be substantial but frugal. The Brothers were labourers, engaged for several hours of every day in arduous toil, they needed support, and were to practice no other abstinence than what the rule of the Church laid upon all; but at the same time they were *poor* labourers, and nothing choice or costly was to be seen on their table—their bodies were to be provided with what was necessary, nothing more.

The next thing to be decided was their dress. Hitherto they had worn the clothes which they had brought with them into the house, but they felt that it would be better to have a distinctive dress, and all the reasons which have led to the universal adoption of a "habit" by religious orders applied equally to their own case. It was not so clear, however, what their habit should be, and after long discussions about it, they came to the conclusion to leave this knotty point entirely to their Superior. He settled nothing for some months, but when winter came, it happened that one day the Mayor of Rheims advised him to provide all his men with a capote, which was a large loose cloak with sleeves, much worn in Champagne, and an excellent protection against cold and wet. De la Salle followed his suggestion, and had the cloaks made long, of a strong coarse material, and black. They were at once adopted as the habit of the community, with a plain black cassock without a girdle, thick, double-soled shoes, and a broad-brimmed hat.

For a name they chose that of "Frères des Écoles Chrétiennes," Brothers of Christian Schools, which was probably soon abbreviated into the well-known title of "Frères Chrétiens," or Christian Brothers, so familiar to us.

The most difficult question of all remained to be decided, viz. that of vows. Should they take vows? if so, what? and for how long?

The Brothers desired the protection of vows, and in their ardour they would have made them life long, but this the prudence of their founder would not allow. It was a joy to him to see their eagerness, but he knew how necessary it was that they should mistrust themselves, and put their resolution to the proof, that they might know whether it was really deep and lasting; and so it was decided that they should take the three vows, of poverty, chastity, and obedience, for three years only, but that they should make them perpetual the following year. Events showed how wise was this delay; of the twelve who were then so eager, only eight were there next year to renew their vows, and then it was judged best again to renew for three years only. The younger members of the Community were not allowed to do even so much as this. They only took the vow of obedience, and that for one year, renewing it year by year till their vocation was assured.

It need hardly be said that De la Salle was the first to take these vows, and the most strict and careful in the observance of them. As a Priest he was already pledged to celibacy, and we have seen how unreservedly he had followed the counsel of holy poverty. Not only had he divested himself of all his worldly goods, but he even sought to be the poorest of his poor Community. He would have the humblest clothing, the coarsest food, and the worst room in the house; his only possessions were a New Testament, a copy of the Imitation, a crucifix and a rosary. To some who remonstrated, as if this was carrying poverty to excess, he replied, "How can you say so? Can you deny that one is rich who possesses the Holy Gospel, and who can draw from thence, whenever he pleases, the treasures of life eternal?" He constantly recommended this virtue of poverty to his Brothers. Later on, when the community had spread, and branch houses were established, one wrote to him to complain of the poverty of his house.

"You are poor," he answered, "so was our Lord, though he might have been rich. Follow His divine pattern. You seem to desire to want for nothing—who would not wish to be poor on this condition? Even the rich would be satisfied with it. Remember, I beg of you, that you have not joined the community in order to be comfortable, but to embrace the state of poverty with its discomforts. You are poor, you say—I am glad of it, for it shows that you are happy. You never were so poor—so much the better, you never had such opportunities for practising virtue."

The vow which seemed most difficult for De la Salle as Superior to practise was that of obedience; it was not likely that he would ever have to render obedience to poor laymen, who were so much beneath him in birth, position and learning. But all his life long he was aiming at this. As soon as ever the Community had taken shape, and the vows had been pronounced, he began to think of laying down the Superiorship. He never gave up this design, and succeeded at last in accomplishing it. Even while Superior he ever sought to take a lowly place; if a master happened to be wanted for a school, he would himself fill the place till another could be found. On such occasions he went regularly twice a day to keep school, took the children to church, brought them back, and spent his whole day in teaching them. This was a great vexation to his family and relations, who could not bear to see him demeaning himself, as they thought, in this manner. Being quite unable to enter into his motives, they attributed his conduct to folly, vanity, and a love of singularity.

They little knew what a continual self-denial his life was, or at what a sacrifice of his natural inclinations he carried on his active and energetic work. All through his busy life his longing was for silence and solitude. He yearned for a life of contemplation alone with God, and he was ever on the watch to catch if it were but a few minutes for retirement and prayer. He had a little room at the top of the house which he kept entirely private, and where he spent all the time he could; but he was seldom left long in peace. Besides attending to the affairs of his Community, he had to receive numerous visits. His growing reputation for sanctity drew many people to him, and he would not refuse to see them, in case his counsels might be helpful to them. He had also to receive visits of curiosity from his former fellow canons and others who wished to judge for themselves concerning the truth of the reports about him. He received all courteously, but did his utmost to escape from these distractions.

In the year 1686 he went into retreat in the convent of Mount Carmel, not far from Rouen. He took every precaution not to be disturbed while there, and did not even leave his address. He left one of the Brothers in charge at Rheims with power to see to everything, but if any real difficulty should arise, he was to write to a nun at Rouen, who would forward the letter. He had hardly reached the place of his retreat, when two Brothers who had charge of the school at Laon, near Rheims, were taken suddenly and dangerously ill. The one whom he had left as his representative at Rheims, went there immediately, but only arrived in time to find one of them at the point of death. In this trouble he wrote to the Superior, who at once gave up his retreat and in three days reached the spot. The disappointment was no vexation to him, for he saw in it the will of God for him, and his only desire was to fulfil that will.

Having no one to place in charge of the school at Laon, he dismissed the children for two months' holiday, and forthwith set out on his return to Rheims with the Brother who had sent for him. They travelled on foot and by night, without any rest. Near midnight De la Salle consented to take a morsel of bread and a glass of wine in a village which they passed through, about four leagues from Rheims. After this slight refection they set out again, and reached Rheims before dawn. As soon as they arrived he sent his companion to bed, and himself prepared for his Mass by meditation and prayer. Prayer was his rest and refreshment.

The death of the schoolmaster at Laon was one of many losses which the Community suffered about this time. Between the year 1681 and 1688 six or seven of the most promising of the Brotherhood were carried off. And in 1683 there had come the news of the death of one who, though not belonging to the Community, had from the first been a devoted friend and adviser of the founder. The Père Barré's life of unceasing good works came to an end, and he rested from his many labours. His counsels had been all along most helpful to De la Salle, and he deeply felt his loss.

This sorrow, added to that caused by the death of so many of his confraternity, seems to have much deepened his desire to lay down the office of Superior, and give himself more to prayer and meditation. He was persuaded that there were in the Community several quite capable of discharging the duties of the Superior, from which he the rather desired to be relieved because he found that the external administration of their affairs tended at times to trouble his relationship to the brethren as their confessor and spiritual director.

He assembled all the Brothers and laid before them his reasons for desiring to be relieved of the burden, reminding them at the same time, that as they must sooner or later have another Superior, it might be as well to elect one, while he the founder was still with them, to help him with his counsels and experience. His arguments prevailed; his resignation was accepted, Frère Henri l'Heureux was elected Superior, and M. de la Salle took his place in the Community as a simple Brother, setting an example to all of the humblest obedience and the strictest regularity. Morning and evening he, with the rest, accused himself of his faults—the very slightest omission he confessed on his knees before them all, and asked for penance. He did not presume to receive a visit, or to open his lips before a stranger, without permission.

He not only rendered obedience to the Superior, but also to every one of the Brothers who had any charge or office in the house. He asked as a favour to be allowed to discharge the lowliest duties, and a visitor coming unexpectedly might have found him sweeping the house, or preparing the vegetables, and washing the dishes under the orders of the Brother who superintended the kitchen.

Being quite aware of the remarks which would be made about his change of position if it came to be publicly known, he desired that it should be kept private, and not made known outside the Community; but his humility and obedience betrayed him. Some persons of distinction called at the house one day to see him, but he told them that he could not speak to them without leave from the Superior, which he said he would go at once and ask for. This took them quite by surprise, and they did not attempt to conceal either their astonishment or their displeasure. The news soon spread in the town, and made a great stir. At last it reached the Archiepiscopal household; the Grand Vicars felt with all the rest of the world that it was a kind of scandal that a Priest, a Doctor of Theology, a former Canon, should be under obedience to a poor lay schoolmaster, and, armed it may be supposed with the Archbishop's authority, they went at once to the house of the Community to right this wrong, by requiring M. de la Salle to resume his place as Superior, and the Frère l'Heureux to return to his obedience. This he was most willing and thankful to do, and De la Salle took up again, without a murmur, those duties of government from which he was not allowed to escape.

Meantime his Institute was growing and developing in unlooked for ways. One day a lad of fifteen came to him and begged to be admitted. De la Salle had never received any one so young before, and did not wish to do so. He felt that at that age there was not physical strength for the strict rule of the society, and that to make exceptions, and grant dispensations, would have a bad effect on the Community. He therefore preferred to receive only those who had attained to man's estate. But this young fellow was so much in earnest, and seemed so well disposed, that he determined to accept him. No sooner had he done so, than three more knocked at the door and asked the same favour. This put it into his mind to form a small community, where the young ones might live apart, and be trained under a less severe rule, and which would serve as a kind of noviciate, or preparation for the other house. Having carefully inquired into the motives and dispositions of the lads, he received them, and established them in an adjoining house, communicating by one door only with the Brothers' house, with separate dormitories, refectory, and class rooms, the kitchen only being in common. Here the four young fellows were placed under the charge of an elderly and experienced Brother. Their rule resembled that of the Brothers, but was modified to suit their age. They had fixed hours for devotion, spiritual reading, prayer, and examination of conscience, and the rest of their time was spent in improving themselves in reading, writing, arithmetic, and singing, with the needful recreation. They wore no habit, but the regularity of their lives, together with the training and instruction which De la Salle delighted to give them, soon stamped the little noviciate with a religious character. It had begun with only four, in the course of two months the number increased to twelve, and thus a real noviciate and preparatory house was established, from which from time to time one and another was passed on to the elder community, and employed in the schools.

Circumstances very soon led to the formation of another supplementary establishment of a rather different kind. The country clergy in the neighbourhood of Rheims hearing of the admirable management of the schools in the towns under the Brothers, began to apply to De la Salle for masters for their schools. The schools in country parishes were worst off of all. The humble position of a schoolmaster in such places, and the very poor provisions that could be made for him, made it extremely difficult to find men to undertake the office, and the clergy who were constantly urged by their Bishops to see to the education of the children in their parishes, found themselves driven to take almost any one who offered himself.

M. de la Salle could not send them any. He had not men enough for the demands of the towns; and besides, he made it a rule not to expose the members of his Community to the trials and temptations of solitude; he always placed two together in charge of a school, and of course little country places could neither support nor find work for two.

The clergy then adopted another plan. They sought out among their parishioners young men of good character, well disposed, and who were willing, if only they could be sufficiently taught themselves, to undertake the office of schoolmasters. Having found some such, they sent them to M. de la Salle, with an earnest request that he would instruct them in the art of teaching, and as far as possible train them after the manner of those who were doing such good work in Rheims and the neighbouring towns.

Neither the men themselves nor the poor clergy who sent them could furnish anything towards their maintenance. For board and lodging, as well as for training and instruction, they looked to the Superior of the Christian Brothers.

He accepted the charge, established them in a separate house, under an experienced Brother, gave them a rule of life especially adapted to their condition, which was to be that of simple, earnest, and devout laymen, with none of the characteristics of the religious life, strictly so-called. They were taught reading and writing, and plain song, that they might be able to help the clergy in the services of the Church. When they had been sufficiently taught, they went back to the villages whence they came, to take charge of the schools.

Thus was formed the first Training College for ordinary secular schoolmasters, and with it the whole machinery of primary education may be said to have been completed. And De la Salle found himself at the head of three distinct establishments, numbering amongst them over fifty persons, all of them looking to him for training, instruction, and maintenance. And to meet the expense of their support he had absolutely nothing; nevertheless, as long as he was at Rheims their wants were all supplied. The blessing of God was upon him, and upon his work.

CHAPTER VIII.

WORK IN PARIS.

1688.

THE year 1688 was an eventful one in the history of M. de la Salle and his Community. In that year he, for the first time, undertook work in Paris. He had long wished to do so; his venerable friend Père Barré, to whose counsels he had so often looked for guidance, had pressed him to go there; and he had once promised M. de la Barmondière, the curé of Saint Sulpice, that he would come and open a school in his parish.

But he was always slow to move, or to take any decided step, without being very plainly called to do so, either by providential circumstances, or by the commands of his superiors. The Archbishop of Rheims was not at first at all inclined to favour his going to Paris. He felt the advantage his Diocese would derive if the Community of the Christian Brothers were permanently established there, and he tried to persuade their founder not to move from Rheims. As an inducement to him to remain, he promised to take upon himself all the expenses of the Community, and to furnish means for extending their work to every parish in the Diocese, on the one only condition, that they should undertake no work outside the Diocese of Rheims.

To this condition M. de la Salle could not consent; he would not tie his own hands, or limit the possible usefulness of his Society in any work to which it might be the will of God to call them; and the offer of pecuniary help was not likely to have much weight with one who had parted with everything in order to cast himself and his followers wholly and without reserve upon Providence for their maintenance.

When the Archbishop found that his mind was made up, he withdrew his objections, and left him free to go wherever he might be called.

But before we enter upon the story of De la Salle's work in Paris, it will be necessary to mention some peculiarities in the management of elementary schools there, as distinguished from those in the country at large, as they were the occasion of great troubles to him; indeed, most of the trials and disappointments of his life grew out of them.

As far back as history can reach there is mention of a school attached to the Cathedral Church of Paris. It is mentioned in the time of Saint Germain, that is about 556. It had been founded by the Bishop, and was conducted by the Canons, one of whom, the Grand Chantre, or Precentor, had the direction of it.

The original object of it was to teach reading and singing, with a view to train children for the due performance of Divine Service, but the benefits of education were extended to all who chose to apply for them.* Paris was of small extent in those days; it clustered round its Cathedral Church, and the School of Notre Dame was sufficient for the needs of the town.

But as the city grew and extended itself, it became necessary to provide more schools. Naturally the new ones, like the first, were begun in connection with the Churches; each collegiate or conventual Church had one; and supplementary schools, under lay teachers of both sexes, appear to have been established in various districts.

In a census of the inhabitants of Paris, taken by Philip le Bel, in the year 1292, for purposes of taxation, eleven schoolmasters and one mistress appear.

A century later the number had increased to sixty-three, forty-one masters and twenty-two mistresses. In the fifteenth century the number of schools had risen to a hundred; a century later there were five hundred; and at the beginning of

* Registre du Chapitre. Arch. nat.

the seventeenth century, the city of Paris, with its forty-three parishes, was divided for the purposes of elementary education, into one hundred and forty-seven districts, in each of which, generally speaking, there was a school for boys and one for girls. The parish of Saint Sulpice alone, which was not much larger in extent than it is now, contained seventeen of these districts, or thirty-four schools.*

The appointment of schoolmasters and mistresses rested wholly with the Precentor of the Cathedral, and was in force for twelve months only. Every year, on the Festival of Saint John Baptist, June 24, their letters of institution (so to speak) were called in, and only renewed if there had been no complaint either as to their general conduct, or the teaching given in their school.

As might be expected, such strict supervision was not acceptable to all, and attempts were not unfrequently made by private individuals to open schools on their own account exempt from all supervision. They were generally started in out-of-the-way places, in the hope of escaping observation; and hence they got the name of bush or hedge schools (écoles buissonières). They were mostly the work of speculating adventurers, who

---

* This extraordinary multiplication of schools seems to have been owing to the fact that class teaching was unknown; each child was taught separately, so that a very small number was as much as a master or mistress could undertake (see chap. xi.).

sought to attract pupils by high-sounding prospectuses. One undertook to teach both Greek and Latin perfectly in three months. But the most elaborate bill of fare was in the prospectus of a man who undertook to teach by himself alone "grammar, rhetoric, philosophy, mathematics, theology, jurisprudence, medicine, mechanics, fortification, geography, heraldry, astronomy, chronology, Roman law, canon law, municipal law, etc."

The Precentor set his face against all such charlatans. The instruction of children was not to be a money speculation. The Parliament supported him in his endeavours to abolish all unsanctioned or hedge schools; acts were passed condemning them, and confirming the authority of the Precentor over all the elementary schools of Paris and its suburbs. Everywhere else the supervision of them was vested in the parochial clergy. The Precentor was the representative of the Cathedral Chapter, which in its turn represented the authority of the Archbishop.

For a long time this authority was undisputed and unopposed; some disturbance was caused by the Protestants in the troublous days of the sixteenth century, but that was soon put down. Later on an attempt was made by the municipal authorities of Paris to get the control of the schools and school teachers into their hands; this was also defeated, but there remained a rankling jealousy between the municipal and the ecclesiastical authorities of Paris, which caused the former to lend their support to a troublesome and factious opposition, arising out of circumstances which are worth mentioning with some detail, as throwing a curious light on the customs of the times.

Before the invention of printing the copying of books and manuscripts was an important and lucrative profession; those who exercised it were under the control of the University, and bore the name of Writers (écrivains). When the art of printing came into general use, their employment, and consequently their earnings, were seriously diminished; but they still existed as a distinct class, and made it their profession to give lessons in writing.

In the year 1570, an error having occurred in some deed, seven of these writers made application to the King, Charles IX., to grant them a monopoly of the verification of all copies of public papers, and also of the right to give instruction in the art of writing.

The Provost of Paris, seeing in this an opportunity of revenge for the defeat he had sustained, in his conflict with the Precentor, seconded their petition, on condition that he should have ex-officio authority over them—should preside at their admission and receive their oaths.

Letters patent were issued in November, 1570, by

which the right was conferred upon the writers, or writing masters (maitres écrivains), to open schools for writing, spelling, and arithmetic.

They were formed into a regular corporation, or guild, for admission to which a residence of three years was required, as well as a strict examination into their moral character and capability, the report of which was laid before the Provost.

The University took alarm at this first intrusion of the civil power into the matter of education, and made some attempts at resistance, but in vain. The letters patent granting these powers and privileges received the sanction of the Parliament.

It might have been expected that the writing masters would have been satisfied with what they had obtained; but no, the permission to teach writing was not enough, unless they could have a complete monopoly of it; and to this end they set themselves to get a prohibition to all other schoolmasters to teach writing in their schools.

The Provost and Municipal Council of Paris were on their side; the Parliament inclined to the side of the University and Church party, who upheld the rights of the schoolmasters. The Provost issued an order that no writing was to be taught except by the writing masters; this was forthwith repealed by Parliament; but a decree was obtained forbidding them to set copies in any words except monosyllables.

This strange and childish dispute actually lasted for a century and a half, and was at last terminated by an Act of Parliament of 23rd of July, 1714, by which it was finally enacted that the masters of elementary schools might teach reading, writing, grammar and arithmetic, but they were not to have separate schools for writing, nor to set copies for their scholars of more than three lines! The writing masters, on the other hand, might teach spelling as well as writing, but they were to have no alphabets, primers, or grammars, in their schools.

To return to De la Salle, and his work. The parish of Saint Sulpice, together with the whole of the Faubourg Saint Germain, had been at one time notorious as one of the worst, if not the very worst, district in Paris; but under the ten years' incumbency of M. Olier, and the earnest unremitting work of the zealous band who formed his Society, its character had been entirely changed, and when he resigned the charge in order to devote himself wholly to the care of the College or Seminary which he had founded there, he left the parish in good order, full of charitable institutions and pious works of all kinds, and as remarkable for all that was good, as it had been notorious for evil.

At the time of which we are speaking thirty years had passed since M. Olier's resignation, but his successors had all been earnest men, trained in his own Community, and the good works of the parish were kept up. Amongst them, free or charity schools for the education of the children of the poor held a prominent place.

It has been stated that the parish of Saint Sulpice already contained the extraordinary number of thirty-four schools, seventeen for boys and seventeen for girls. But these were paying schools, and it was therefore thought necessary to add to the number seven charity schools, each having its own district attached, for children whose parents were too poor to pay. These schools were under the supervision of a charitable association in the parish, the members of which undertook to visit the schools regularly; they inquired into the progress of the children, and their behaviour, took note of their attendance, looked after the absent ones, and generally superintended the work.

No better provision could have been made, and all would have been well, but for the great difficulty in getting masters. It was almost impossible to get men sufficiently capable, and at the same time of good character; and in consequence, one school after another had to be given up, till in the year 1688, instead of the seven free schools established by M. Olier, there remained only one, in which two hundred children were gathered together. It was held in a house in the Rue Princesse, belonging to the curé, and next door to the Seminary of Saint Sulpice, and it had been placed under the charge of the Abbé Compagnon, one of the clergy of that Seminary. He had one assistant, a young fellow who was inexperienced and untrained, and the children were entirely beyond control. The school was a scene of uproar and confusion, and misbehaviour of all kinds, and it became a nuisance to the neighbourhood. M. Compagnon found the management of it quite too much for him, and having heard of M. de la Salle's work at Rheims, he wrote to him, and with urgent entreaties asked him to send him a master.

It was De la Salle's rule never to send out one of the Brothers alone, and also never to undertake work in a parish at the request of any one but the Incumbent himself. He therefore replied that he was quite ready to send two Brothers, if M. de la Barmondière desired it. After a good deal of harassing delay, which seems to have been caused by the Abbé's wish to keep the arrangements as much as possible in his own hands, a cordial invitation came from the Curé, reminding De la Salle of the promise made many years before, that he would open a school in the parish of Saint Sulpice, and begging him to come at once, or send two masters.

His way being thus made plain, he lost no time, but set out immediately with two of his Brothers, and arrived in Paris on the Eve of Saint Mathias, the 23rd of February, 1688. He and the Brothers were lodged in the house in the Rue Princesse, and they forthwith took charge of the school. De la Salle soon found that he had entered upon a work which was to cause him much trouble and annoyance.

The wonderful improvement which in a short time became evident in the school, roused the jealousy of the very man who had been so anxious to obtain his help, and, yielding to the evil spirit of envy which possessed him, the Abbé Compagnon, instead of being a helper, became as far as he could a hinderer of the work; and at last, finding that it still prospered, and that the contrast became more and more striking between the school, as it was under his charge, and its conditions under De la Salle, he brought a slanderous accusation of a very grave kind against him. He chose his opportunity for spreading this evil report, when there was a meeting of the ladies of the Assemblée de Charité, the district visitors as we should call them, at the house of the Curé, and made his statement with such positiveness of circumstantial detail that even M. de la Barmondière could not help believing him.

De la Salle knew the false reports which were being circulated about him, and he could not but be conscious of a change in the manner of his friend the Curé towards him; but he took no notice, and made no attempts to prove his innocence; leaving his cause in the hands of God, he suffered in silence, and occupied himself entirely with the children of the school.

M. de la Barmondière was surprised that he made no attempt to refute the charges brought against him, and he seems to have taken it as a conclusive proof of his guilt, for he determined to dismiss him and the Brothers whom he had brought with him; but as he did not wish to expose him to public disgrace he sent him word by his curate, that when the time for the school holidays came, he had better leave Paris quietly of his own accord.

M. de la Salle accepted this most unjust judgment, and all the disappointment it involved, without a word of remonstrance; he asked no questions, only prepared to depart. But when he went to take leave of M. de la Barmondière, there was something in his bearing and manner which convinced him that he could not be guilty of the crimes of which he was accused; a judicial inquiry was instituted, and his innocence was clearly proved. When he was asked if he could explain the Abbé Compagnon's behaviour, he replied, that he knew nothing about it, and the only favour he would ask for himself was, that he might be told of any faults which were seen in his conduct, and that he might receive such counsels as he had need of.

The school went on prospering, and the numbers increased so fast, that it became necessary to open another school, and two more masters were sent for from Rheims, for whose maintenance the curé of Saint Sulpice made himself responsible.

But this success brought trouble of another kind. The schoolmasters of the neighbourhood, who earned their living by their profession, became alarmed; they feared that children who could pay would be drawn away from their schools to attend the Brothers' school, and so their gains would be diminished. They therefore combined together to try to put a stop to the work. They took legal proceedings against the Brothers, and so began a strife, which went on at intervals, with varying success, being carried from one court to another, for fifteen years.

Their first appeal was to the Precentor, whose position of authority over all schools except the charity schools, has been already explained. He, hearing only the schoolmasters' representations of the case, gave his judgment against the Christian Brothers. But though M. de la Salle would make no defence in a cause which concerned himself alone, it was different when the work which he desired to do for God and the Church was hindered; after a day spent with his Brothers in fasting and prayer, he went to the Precentor's court and pleaded his cause with such effect that the judgment was reversed, and he was left free to carry on his work, for a time, in peace.

The anxieties caused by this and other troubles, added to the privations which he endured, partly from poverty, and partly from his love of hardships and mortifications, affected De la Salle's health. Towards the end of the year 1690 he made a journey to Rheims on foot, as his custom was; when he arrived there his strength gave way, and he was obliged to take to his bed. The doctors ordered complete rest, care, and nourishing food, to restore his strength. All these he might have had in his grandmother's house, who was still living, and loved him dearly; but he would not leave the Community or take any indulgence beyond what their rule allowed.

As soon as he got better he insisted on returning to Paris. His doctor and his friends did all they could to prevent him, but he would go. The fatigues of the journey brought on a relapse, and for six weeks the illness was so severe that there seemed to be hardly any hope of his recovery. But the earnest prayers offered up without ceasing for him were heard, he was restored to his usual health, and immediately resumed his accustomed habits. His time at Rheims had been interrupted by illness, so that he had not been able to attend to the business for which he had gone there. He therefore went back as soon as he was sufficiently recovered, leaving the Frère l'Heureux in charge of those at Paris. This was the man who had been once elected Superior in his place; he was much above the average in intelligence, earnestness, and devotion, and De la Salle quite looked to him as his successor; in preparation for which he wished him to receive Holy Orders, and he was at this time preparing for his Ordination, which was to take place almost immediately.

While De la Salle was at Rheims he received a letter telling him that l'Heureux was ill of a fever. Next day there came a worse account, and soon after so bad a one that he set out for Paris immediately, but arrived to find his much loved son in his grave. This was one of the greatest sorrows of his life. When he came to the house and heard that the Frère l'Heureux was no more, he could not refrain from tears; but he soon recovered himself, and bore this afflicting stroke without a murmur. It had, however, the effect of greatly changing his plans. He had not only counted on putting l'Heureux in his own place, but his purpose had been to have one of the Brothers in each house in Holy Orders, to say Mass for them and hear their confessions. But this death came to him as a providential warning not to do so. Objections which had not occurred to him before rose up in his mind. He felt that the combination of clerical and lay Brothers might be a source of jealousy and disunion; that all would want to rise to the dignity of the Priesthood, and would hold in contempt the humble work of the school; preaching and study would have more attractions than the thankless labour of teaching poor children, and the whole character and speciality of the community would be lost. These considerations led him to determine never to receive a Priest into the community, and also to make it a rule in his Institute that none of the Brothers should ever be ordained, and as a further safeguard, he added another, that they should not learn Latin. To this rule he never consented to allow any exceptions.

CHAPTER IX.

FIRST HOUSE AT VAUGIRARD.

1688-1694.

WHEN De la Salle came to Paris in 1688, he left behind him at Rheims three flourishing communities. In the principal house there were sixteen Brothers, not counting the two whom he took with him; the training college for country schoolmasters contained thirty men, and there were fifteen lads in the little noviciate. But the absence of the founder seemed to bring a blight upon all.

The Brother who had been left in charge during his absence, was lacking in judgment and in sympathy. Through his mismanagement eight of the sixteen Brothers left the community, and for four years not one came to supply their place. The country schoolmasters were by degrees drafted off to the villages whence they came, to take charge of the schools, and as M. de la Salle was no longer there to inspire confidence, the country clergy ceased to send men for training, and this excellent institution came to an end. The young novices, too, were evidently suffering so much for want of his fatherly care and teaching, that he sent for them to come to him to Paris. It was too plain that as yet he was the life and soul of his Institute, its stay and support in all its departments—necessary, in short, to its very existence. When he was present it grew and developed in spite of obstacles; when he was absent it languished, and if his absence was prolonged, it seemed in danger of perishing entirely. This personal dependence on himself was a cause of great disquietude to De la Salle. He knew that no institution could have any permanence which so hung upon one individual; and it was a distress to him also, because it wounded his humility.

Another care which weighed heavily upon him was the condition of the Brothers who were in charge of schools, at Rheims, and in other towns. The health of many of them was failing, from over work and privations. Shut up from morning to night in small close schoolrooms, constantly engaged in a thankless and wearing toil, badly fed, and poorly lodged, their strength seemed to be giving way; and their Superior, who watched over them with a father's love and tenderness, saw that some plan must be adopted to provide a place where they might come for rest when needful. And it was not only their bodily health which needed restoration; many of them had lost their early fervour;

they had grown lax in the observance of their rule; they were not yet sufficiently settled in the religious life to bear up against the temptations and distractions incidental to their position, and to their necessary contact with the world around them. It was plainly necessary that from time to time they should gather round their saintly founder, in order that the flame of their devotion might be rekindled by contact with the fire which glowed in his fervent soul; and so they might be led on, under his guidance, towards that type of Christian perfection which he had all along set before them, and which he had himself so wonderfully attained.

With this object, De la Salle hired a house at the entrance of the village of Vaugirard, near Paris; it was poor and badly built, but it stood apart, with a garden belonging to it, in a healthy situation, and was well suited to become a second nursery of his Institute. He occupied it for seven years, during which all the Brothers spent their vacations there, and those in Paris, whenever they had a holiday, came out to him. It was a house of rest for the sick and weary, and postulants sojourned there for a time, to make proof of their vocation, and learn their duties.

It was in the year 1691 that M. de la Salle first took possession of the house, and it was autumn, the time of general school holidays throughout the country, so that he was able to assemble all the

Brothers from Rheims and the neighbouring towns, as well as from Paris; and as it was long since he had had any intercourse with them, he kept them with him till the end of the year, supplying their places for a few weeks by some of the masters who had been trained for the country parishes, but who could very well help temporarily in the towns.

When he had thus gathered all his children round him, he began by giving them a ten days' Retreat, which alone did much to renew their fervour; but he followed it up by earnest exhortations and personal dealings with each one of them, warning, rebuking, checking their faults and failings, and endeavouring by all means to develop the special virtues and graces in each of their characters.

He was most anxious to associate two of them very closely with himself, that they might be the confidants of all his thoughts and plans, and might share the burden of the superiorship with him.

He chose the two who seemed to him fittest for this office, and, at his suggestion, they bound themselves by a solemn vow to act in cordial union with him and each other, and to work together till their lives' end for the Society. Sad to say, one of these proved faithless, and eventually turned out very badly. But the good father had no presentiment of this grief; he was full of confidence in his "threefold cord," and, cheered by the sense of companionship in his cares, he turned all his attention to the improvement and perfecting of the Brothers whom he had gathered round him. They were full of good will, and his influence and example had their usual effect. By the end of the year they were different men, penitent, humble, docile, recollected; and their Superior felt that he could let them return to their several posts without anxiety. But as a protection for the future, he made it a rule that they should write to him every month, opening their hearts freely and fully to him, and telling him all their troubles and difficulties. He also visited them when he could, and as long as he had the house at Vaugirard, he caused them all to assemble there once a year, to make a retreat of ten days, and to follow strictly for a month the exercises of the noviciate.

This house also served as a Home for the novices. The ranks of the Brothers had been so thinned by death and by desertion, that there were many vacant places to fill, and on the 1st of November, 1692, De la Salle gave the habit to five novices, and one serving Brother.

It was no easy life which these young men came to make trial of. In truth it was hard from necessity as well as from choice. The house was poor, the windows were badly fitted and let in the cold, and even in the depth of winter they had no fires. Their food was scanty and often insufficient; they lived on the broken victuals which were given them in charity. Every day one of the Brothers went to

Paris to collect such scraps for their dinner, and even this poor provision was sometimes taken from them, by starving men who waylaid and robbed them on their return. When this happened the community had to do without their dinners.

Poorly lodged, and poorly fed, they were also poorly clothed—patched garments, worn out hats, and shoes which a beggar would not care to accept, composed their costumes; and yet amid all these surroundings of utter poverty, their countenances shone with a radiant serenity which spoke of inward peace, and even joyousness.

It was quite necessary that the discipline of their noviciate should be hard. Young men brought up in all the comforts of family life, in easy or even wealthy circumstances, frequently offered themselves to join the brotherhood; it was essential that they should first make trial, by actual experience, of the privations and hardships of the life which they desired to embrace. In no other way could the reality of their vocation be effectually tested. De la Salle had had some experience of the mischief which may be done in a community by those who enter it under a mistake as to their vocation, and he was deeply impressed with the need there was of the most watchful care to admit none but those whose devotion was deep and sincere, and who had strength, both physical and moral, to bear the strictness of the rule.

The house at Vaugirard might be likened to a net which gathered fish of every kind, and there was need of great discrimination to judge of their quality, and reject those which were not worth keeping. Many came and asked for admission to the noviciate; some were drawn by curiosity; others by unrest and dissatisfaction with themselves, their lives, and their surroundings; and some by the hope of finding a maintenance. There were, indeed, amongst the applicants not a few whose motive was a real love of God, and desire to work for His glory; but even with these there was a need of caution, as it did not follow that they were called to serve Him in that particular work. De la Salle seems to have had a special gift for discerning the true vocations amongst all these; he was not often mistaken; and the severity of the rule was a test which no false or secondary motives could stand. Of the first twelve who were admitted to the noviciate, only two remained to the end faithful members of the community. And yet, notwithstanding this careful sifting, the numbers soon rose to thirty-five.

In spite of his poverty De la Salle managed to support this large family, or it might more truly be said, he asked for their daily bread, and it was given. The expenses were necessarily great, and they were much increased by the number of persons who passed through the house, without joining the community. But no one was refused; the door was ever open, and they were as free to come in as to go out. Moreover, Vaugirard being so conveniently near Paris, the house of the Christian Brothers became a sort of hotel for any clergy who happened to be journeying thither, and a place of resort for those who had nowhere else to go. Stranger Priests often asked a lodging there, and were made welcome to stay as long as they conformed to the rules of the house.

In 1693 there was a terrible famine in Paris and the neighbourhood, and the community of the Christian Brothers suffered sadly. More than once they were absolutely without food, but the Superior never lost his cheerful serenity; he spared no efforts to provide for them, but when he had done his best, he dismissed all anxious care, and took cheerfully whatever came. He fared no better than the rest; they had nothing to bear which he did not himself share to the full; indeed, he took more than his share of hardships and privations. At last things came to such a pass that they were in actual danger, not only of starvation but of violence. The environs of Paris were infested by starving marauders who, as has been said, sometimes seized the poor supplies of food on their way to Vaugirard, and, as the house was lonely and unprotected, De la Salle thought it best to carry his family back to Paris, and establish them in the house in the Rue Princesse which he had occupied on his first arrival.

Great distress and dearth still prevailed, and even here it happened more than once that the Brothers assembled in the refectory, and sang their Benedicite round an empty table, or dined on a bouillon of herbs. Happily none of them fell sick during the time of these terrible privations. In the year 1694 the famine abated, and De la Salle returned to Vaugirard with his Community, leaving nine Brothers in charge of schools in Paris.

The sufferings they had gone through together seemed only to have bound the hearts of the brethren closer to their Community and to its venerable founder, and on their return to Vaugirard they implored him to allow them to make their vows perpetual, instead of for three years only, as heretofore. "Why," they said, "should we be bound to our God, only as labouring men are to the masters whom they serve? At the end of the year they are free, and may take up with another master; our condition, as we are now, is like theirs; when the time of our vows has expired, we find ourselves, to our great peril, at liberty, a liberty which too often leads to irregularities, and may be our ruin. If we made our sacrifice complete, by vows of perpetual obligation, God would accept our purpose, and strengthen us to abide by it."

As usual, De la Salle did not at once yield to this request. He exhorted them to constant and

Vow of Perpetual Obligation.   117

earnest prayer, that they might know the will of God, and when the Trinity Season drew near he assembled twelve of the Brothers in retreat. They were those on whose steadfastness he thought he could most rely. He himself conducted their retreat, and set before them the gravity of the engagement to which they desired to bind themselves, and warned them of the great peril of taking upon themselves more than they were able to bear.

Having taken all possible pains to guard them against over-boldness and self-confidence, and finding them still of the same mind, at last he consented to their wish, and on Trinity Sunday he first consecrated himself for life to the work which he had undertaken, and then received from each one of them the vow of life-long steadfastness and obedience. The original copy of the formula of their vow may still be seen among the archives of the society, in the handwriting of Jean Baptiste de la Salle, and with his signature. It is as follows:—

"Most holy Trinity, Father, Son, and Holy Ghost, prostrate in deepest reverence before Thine infinite and adorable Majesty, I consecrate myself wholly to Thee, to seek Thy glory in all ways possible to me, or to which Thou shalt call me. And to this end, I, Jean Baptiste de la Salle, Priest, promise and vow to unite myself to, and abide in society with, the Brothers (here follow twelve names), and in union and association with them to hold free schools in any place whatsoever (even though in order to do so, I should have to beg for alms, and live on dry bread), or to do in the said Society any work which may be appointed for me, whether by the Community, or by the Superior who shall have the direction of it. For which reason I promise and vow obedience as well to the Society itself as to the Superior of it. And these vows of association with, and steadfastness in, the said Community, and of obedience, I promise to keep inviolable during my whole life; in witness whereof I have signed. Done at Vaugirard, this sixth day of June, being the Feast of the Most Holy Trinity, in the year 1694.

"(Signed)   DE LA SALLE."

When this important step had been taken, De la Salle thought the time was come at last, when he might fulfil his long-cherished wish, and retire from the office of Superior. So the very next day he called the Brothers together, and tried to convince them that it would be for the advantage of the society that he should do so. He told them, amongst other things, that they ought now to seek by all means to make the bond which united them to one another so strong that neither the world nor the devil should be able to break it. That for this they must put their trust in God, and not lean upon any man. That he was only a poor helpless priest, who three years ago had been at the gates of death, and might be brought down there again at any moment; that if he died, they would find themselves without a head, and their ecclesiastical superiors might appoint one over them who neither knew them nor their traditions, and who might want to change their rules, and alter the spirit of the society. Therefore it would be well that whilst he was still with them they should elect another Superior, and that he should be one of themselves, so that the difference of position between the Priestly office and their own might not be a cause of disunion.

The Brethren did not enter into the force of these reasons. They remembered their former experience, and they had no mind again to put the flock above the shepherd, the sons above the Father, the penitents above the confessor.

De la Salle saw that they were not convinced, and he renewed his arguments more eloquently than before. Finding that they made no answer, he was in hopes that he had persuaded them, and before taking the votes he made them spend half an hour in prayer for the guidance of the Holy Ghost. They then proceeded to the election, and it was found that every vote, without a single exception, had been given for him.

Disappointed, but touched, he gently reproached them with disregard to the highest interests of the Community and an inordinate esteem for himself; and he besought them to try once more, hoping that in answer to his prayers they might be guided to make another choice. They consented to do so, but again the result was the same. The Brothers then urged him to accept their unanimous decision as the voice of God. At his death they said it would be time enough to put one of themselves at their head. Till then he must not refuse to bear the burden so plainly laid upon him by God Himself.

The venerable man lifted his eyes to Heaven, and meekly submitted to what appeared indeed to be the will of God; but he was so persuaded of the danger there would be to the Society in time to come if the Superior should be in Holy Orders that he made all the Brothers sign a declaration to the effect that although they had unanimously elected him as their Superior for his life, they would never after his death make a Priest head of the Community, but would choose their Superior from amongst the Brethren themselves.

This document is dated Vaugirard, the seventh of June, 1694, and signed by the same twelve who with the Superior had signed the vow of perpetual steadfastness and obedience.

CHAPTER X.

THE RULE.

A TIME of comparative tranquillity in the retirement of Vaugirard followed the events related in the last chapter, and was employed by De la Salle in bringing into definite and permanent shape the Rule of his Community, which he had roughly sketched out at Rheims fifteen years before. During those years it had been tried and acted upon; every member of the Community was perfectly acquainted with its details, but he would not put it forth as the established Rule, without the fullest re-consideration of every point, accompanied by long prayer and fasting, nor even then, without consultation with the brethren. When he had written it out, he called together all the elder members of the Community, and put it into their hands, to be criticised, corrected, added to, if they saw need. They knew that they were perfectly at liberty to make any changes which they thought desirable, and that it would be no offence in the eyes of the founder, to do so; but they found nothing to alter, and returned the copy to him without a single word of correction. The form as at this time drawn up by him, has remained the Rule of the Society, without any material alteration to the present time.

The first article sets forth the end and object of the Society in the following words:—

"The Institute of the Frères des Écoles Chrétiennes is a society, the profession of whose members is, to hold schools gratuitously. The object of this Institute is to give a Christian education to children, and it is for this purpose that schools are held, in order that the masters, who have charge of the children from morning to night, may bring them up to lead good lives, by instructing them in the mysteries of our holy Religion, and filling their minds with Christian maxims, while they give them such an education as is fitting for them.

"This Institute is very greatly needed, because working people and the poor, who are generally but little instructed themselves, and are obliged to spend the whole day in working for their living and that of their children, cannot themselves give them the teaching which is necessary for them. It has been with a view to provide these advantages for the children of the poor, and of labouring men, that the Institution of the Christian Schools has been founded.

"The disorderly lives of the working classes and of the poor are generally attributable to the fact that they have been badly brought up, and suffered to run wild in their childhood; and this evil it is almost impossible to repair in their more advanced years, because bad habits are very difficult to break, and are hardly ever quite cured, however great the pains which are taken to reform them. It is easy, therefore, to see the importance and usefulness of the Christian Schools, since to guard against these disorderly ways and their evil consequences is the principal fruit to be hoped for from their institution."

It is evident from these words that the primary end which the Founder of the Society of the Christian Schools had in view was to bring up the children of the people in the fear and love of God, as true Christians and faithful sons of the Church, being fully persuaded that this was the only effectual way to make them good citizens and useful members of society. But it must not be supposed that religion was taught in his schools to the neglect of secular learning. Far from it. We shall see by-and-by that out of six hours and a half of school time only one half-hour was given to distinctly religious instruction; this was the last half-hour of the afternoon school. The children were also taken to church in the forenoon, which would probably occupy another half-hour, so that one hour out of six and a half was taken for religious training and instruction, the other five given to the ordinary course of secular learning. And the careful and minute directions which De la Salle drew up for the guidance of the Brothers in the conduct of their schools show that while he held religious teaching to be the foundation of all education, and made a religious spirit to pervade everything, the instruction of the children in reading, writing, and arithmetic was most carefully attended to, and effectually done.

In making religious teaching the basis of his system, De la Salle was in direct contradiction to the modern secular spirit which would fain banish all religion from schools; but in two other points, which he also insisted upon as essential, he only forestalled the principles of later times.

1. By making the schools absolutely free, he brought education within reach of every child in the land, however poor his parents might be. And this he did, not by a heavy tax, which, while professing to provide education for those who are unable to pay for it, only lays the burden on the people in another form, but by a *bonâ fide* gratuitous education, given for the love of God, by men who have voluntarily bound themselves to a life of poverty, and therefore require only the barest necessaries of life, and who are pledged by a solemn vow never to receive any kind of remuneration for their service.

2. The other principle which bears a superficial, but only a superficial, resemblance to modern theories was that the teaching was to be entirely in the hands of laymen. As we have already seen no ecclesiastic was permitted to enter the Society, and no member of the Community was allowed to take Holy Orders, nor even to put on a surplice, or discharge any Church office or function what-

ever. But they were none the less Ministers of Christ, full of devotion, deeply penetrated with the Christian faith, and well versed in the Holy Scriptures. Their Rule says :—

"The Brothers of this Society will have a very deep reverence for the Holy Scriptures, and in token of it they will always carry about them a copy of the New Testament, and will pass no day without reading a portion of it, in faith, respect, and veneration for the Divine Words which it contains. They will look upon it as their primary and principal Rule."

"The Brothers of this Society will do everything in a spirit of faith, and in all their actions they will set before them God's holy will and commandments; they will reverence them in all things, and they will take heed to order their own conduct according to them."

The spirit of the Society and of its work is thus set forth :—

"The spirit of the Institute consists in a burning zeal for the instruction of children, that they may be brought up in the fear and love of God, and led to preserve their innocence, where they have not already lost it; to keep them from sin, and to instil into their minds a great horror of evil, and of everything that might rob them of their purity."

"In order to maintain and abide in this spirit, the Brothers of the Society shall labour continually by prayer, by teaching, by vigilance, and by their own good example in the school, to promote the salvation of the children entrusted to them, by bringing them up in a truly Christian spirit, that is to say according to the rules of the Holy Gospel."

Such being the tone and spirit in which the work was to be done, it is plain that a very different stamp of workmen was required from that of ordinary schoolmasters, however well trained in the usual routine of school keeping.

To form such men was the great work to which Jean Baptiste de la Salle's life had been devoted. We have seen how, without any natural predisposition to the kind of thing, his mind was first drawn to it, by what might be called accidental circumstances; how step by step it grew under his hand, till his Institute had assumed the completely developed form of a Religious Order, and we have learned something of his method of training and moulding the rough—often very rough—material which came into his hands, into the form which he had conceived as the highest type of a Christian schoolmaster. Some further light will be thrown upon it by the extracts from the Rules which follow.

The training was of necessity long and systematic, and this was provided for by the noviciate. Young men were received at the age of sixteen or seventeen, or even younger, but they were not allowed to bind themselves in any way to the Society, till they had made full trial of the life, and of the duties which they would have to undertake. Nothing can exceed the care with which the young novices are guarded from joining the Community hastily, or without the fullest deliberation and experience.

"Those Brothers who have not attained the age of twenty-five years, shall only be allowed to take the vows for three years. They shall renew them every year for the same period, until they are accepted, and admitted to take the perpetual vows.

"Those who have reached the age of twenty-five, shall not be admitted to take the perpetual vows, until after they have taken them for three years.

"No one shall ever be allowed to take the vows, even for three years, until he has been at least two years in the Society, and has had one year's experience of the noviciate, and one year's teaching in the schools."

The vows were five in number :—

1. "The vow of poverty obliges them to part with all property in this world, and is a promise made to Almighty God never to possess anything of their own. By virtue of this vow they can never accept or receive anything whatsoever, to have, or to use, or to dispose of in any way, without the permission of their Superior.

2. "The vow of chastity binds them to abstain from everything which is contrary to chastity, in thought, word, affection, or deed.

"3. The vow of obedience pledges them to obey the Superior, the Directors whom he may appoint, and the community itself in its corporate capacity.

"4. By the vow of steadfastness, they promise to abide steadfastly in the Society for the period of time for which they take the vow.

"5. By the vow of giving gratuitous instructions to children, they bind themselves to take all possible pains to teach them well, and to bring them up Christianly. And they promise neither to ask nor to accept, from the scholars, or from their parents, anything, be it what it may, either as a gift, or in any other form of renumeration whatsoever."

Like all other religious Orders, the Institute of the Frères des Écoles Chrétiennes partakes of the nature of a republic, and also of a monarchy. It is governed by a Superior General, elected in a general Chapter composed of certain *ex officio* members, and a fixed number of delegates from the several Branch houses. Great care is taken to secure the due election of these electors. This Superior, who is appointed for life, has associated with him certain assistants, who form his council and help him in the government. They live in the same house, discuss with him all questions which may arise, give him their support and assistance when necessary, and act as his secretaries.

Every branch house has at its head a Frère Directeur, or Superior, of its own, appointed by the Superior General, from whom he receives authority and powers for the government of the house. His authority is not, however, without check and counterpoise, and very careful precautions were taken against its abuse.

Every house was visited once a year by a Brother, chosen for this office by the Superior General. To him the Director had to give an account of his administration, and the visitor reported to the Superior on the state of the house, and on any matter which needed reform or correction. During the life of the founder this visitation was most frequently made by himself, and only when he was unable to go, by Brothers in whom he had the fullest confidence, and who were accredited by him. Several letters written by him for this purpose are still extant. Another protection against any misrule on the part of the Directors was provided by the rule that each Brother wrote at least once in every two months to the Superior.

This slight outline may suffice for what may be called the political constitution of the Society. We must now pass on to the rule of daily life:—

4.30 is the hour of rising at all seasons, winter and summer.

5. They spend a quarter of an hour in vocal prayer; then the subject of their meditation is read, and mental prayer goes on till 6.

6. They attend Mass; after which they read, write, or study the catechism, according to directions received.

7.15. Breakfast in common in the refectory. After breakfast they spend a short time in prayer in their oratory, as a preparation for their school work, and to ask of our Lord to fill them with His Spirit, that they may have grace to lead the children whom they teach to Him. Then they disperse to their several schools.

At 8 the morning schools open, and go on till 11. During this time the children are taken to church and back.

11.30. The Brothers make particular examination of conscience. This is followed by dinner, and after dinner recreation till one o'clock.

1. They assemble again in the oratory for prayer; after which they depart to their various schools, as in the forenoon.
1.30. The afternoon schools open and last till 5.
4. The catechism is taught for half an hour.
4.30. The children repeat reverently and distinctly their evening prayer, and sing some verses of a hymn, after which they are dismissed. After school, the brothers assemble in the oratory to examine their consciences as to faults they may have committed in school time. If they have any time to spare they study the catechism.
5.30. The bell rings for spiritual reading in preparation for mental prayer, which follows it immediately. The reading always begins with half a page of the New Testament, read upon their knees.
6. Mental prayer for half an hour; after which they confess one to another any faults which they are conscious of having committed in the day.
6.30. Supper. During all the meals there is reading. At breakfast it is always from the founder's manual on the management of schools. At dinner and supper they read from the Old and New Testaments, the lives of the Saints, or the Imitation of Jesus Christ. Recreation follows after supper.

8. Study of the catechism for half an hour.

8.30. Evening prayers are said in the oratory, and the subject of the next day's meditation is read.

9. The bell rings, and all retire to the dormitory, and are in bed by 9.15.

Such was to be the time-table of their ordinary working day. It will be found that seven hours are allowed for sleep, four hours are allotted to prayer and religious exercises, six hours and a half to school work, two to private study, and two and a half to meals and recreation. On Sundays, attendances at Divine Service, and catechetical teaching take the place of school work, and they have an additional time for recreation.

For a life of such constant and hard labour it was needful that physical strength should be sustained, and not weakened by austerities. No bodily mortifications were enjoined beyond the usual observance of the Friday and other fasts of the Church. Their discipline consisted in spiritual mortifications. Of these there was no lack; their separation from the world around them, their poverty, and the inevitable hardships which it entailed, their obedience to rule, and to the commands of their Superior; in short, the faithful keeping of their vows furnished in itself abundant opportunity for the mortification of the natural man.

The Rule was strict as to their separation from the world around them.

"The Brothers shall have no communication with persons outside the Community, without a manifest necessity, and then only with the permission of the Director. They will honour all men with whom they have to do, without attaching themselves in friendship to any one. They will never pay visits of civility, nor try to induce others to visit them. They will receive visits as seldom as possible."

Even amongst themselves, particular friendships are forbidden, while brotherly love towards all is enjoined.

"The Brothers shall have a hearty affection for one another, but they shall give no sign or token of special attachment to one above another, out of reverence for our Lord, Whom they should honour equally in all, as bearing Him within them, and being guided by His Spirit."

The bearing of the vow of poverty on the details of daily life, is thus unfolded by the Rule :—

"No brother shall possess anything as his own; everything shall be in common in each house, even the clothes and other things necessary for the use of the Brothers.

"The Brothers shall own nothing for their proper use except a New Testament, a copy of the Imitation of Jesus Christ, a rosary, to which shall be attached a crucifix, which may be of copper, and a small portfolio. These things shall be given them during their Noviciate, by him whose office it is to provide for the needs of the Society.

"The poverty of the Brothers shall always appear in their clothing; at the same time their garments must be decent, *i.e.* not in rags. They shall wear no hat or habit, cloak or shoes, but what are according to the Rule.

"The Brothers shall possess nothing. If they have any property they shall make it over to their relations, and retain no interest in it whatever."

To the mortifications of poverty were added those of an exact obedience, such as implies a complete surrender of their own will, and submission to that of their Superiors, in which they see the will of God Himself.

"They shall do nothing without permission, no matter how small and trifling the thing may be, in order that they may be sure of doing the Will of God in all things."

To do the will of God is the final end and object of the Institute.

CHAPTER XI.

THE MANUAL.

As soon as the Rule of his Society was definitely settled and he had thus provided for the ordering and perfecting of the lives and characters of the Brothers, the founder turned his attention to their work; that is, he set about writing manuals for their guidance in the management of their schools, in which he might embody and hand down for the benefit of the Community in years to come, those rules and methods both of general management and of teaching, which he had first struck out for himself, and had afterwards proved by long experience to be most fruitful in good results.

Before his time the only method of instruction in elementary schools, was individual teaching of each child. One by one the scholars were called up by the master to be taught singly, so that in a school, say of twenty-four boys, supposing five minutes to be spent upon each, it would take two hours to give a lesson all round, while all the other scholars would be left to themselves for an hour and fifty-five minutes. How three and twenty boys would be likely to spend this time, even though they might have lessons set and books before them, need not be described.

Those who have to do with elementary schools nowadays are so accustomed to class-teaching, that it would probably never occur to them as anything but the natural and obvious way of giving a lesson to a large number of children, whereas it was, in fact, invented by the genius of one man. The founder of the Christian schools first began it in France, about a hundred years before anything of the kind was introduced into England.

De la Salle wrote various books on different branches of education, but that which deserves special notice was his work on the general management of schools, "Conduite à l'usage des Écoles Chrétiennes." This he drew up, as has been said, soon after the Rule, probably about the year 1695; copies of it in manuscript were given to all Brothers in charge of schools; it seems to have been widely circulated, and in constant use, but was never printed during his life. In 1717, when he ceased to be Superior, he was asked to revise the book, as it had been found to need some slight alterations. He then went over all points carefully, and the earliest printed edition, dated 1720, a year after his death, is probably an exact copy of the form in which he left it. It has been the manual and *vade mecum* of all the Christian Brothers ever since; it has been read through twice a year in every one of their houses, and has guided the management of all their schools.

The last edition was published in 1860 by the then Superior General, the venerable Frère Philippe, who in his preface explains that certain modifications of the original had become necessary, since "it is evident that a book of this kind can never assume a form which is to be final." This is plain: the lapse of time, increased experience, altered circumstances, different requirements, fresh needs, not to speak of legislative restrictions, all these require to be met by a certain elasticity and power of adaptation, which is itself a sign of the vigorous life of an institution. But the book is the same in all its main lines, and even where it has been found needful to alter some of the details, the principles and the spirit which pervades it are the same.

The experience of centuries has added but little to what he had laid down, guided by quick insight and deep practical study of the subject, coupled with earnest devotion to it, as the work specially given him by God.

The manual is very comprehensive; treating of all points in the management of elementary schools. Such as time-tables, subjects to be taught, the manner of teaching them, books to be used, the classing of the children, the best way of dealing with different characters, the rules which should guide a master in giving rewards and punishments, the importance of regular attendance, and the best means of promoting it, these and many other points are dealt with in detail, and with great practical wisdom. Directions are also given about the furniture of the schoolroom, the height of the desks and of the benches, the kind of ink bottles, pictures for the walls, the best arrangement for light and air, etc.

It may be doubted whether the long and elaborate codes which issue from our Education Department, or from the bureau of the Minister of Public Instruction in France, contain as much practical good sense as this small 12mo volume of 270 pages. A Brother sent to open a school, with this manual in his pocket, knows what directions to give to a builder or a carpenter, and what to order of the bookseller and other tradesmen, besides being provided with counsels of a graver kind as to the graces specially to be cultivated in himself, and the faults he should watch against. Some extracts from it will best show its value; they are taken from the edition of 1720.

On the subject of religious teaching—

"The masters will take such great care in the instruction of all their scholars, that not one shall be left in ignorance, at least of the things which a Christian ought to believe and do. And to the end that they may not neglect a thing of such great importance, they will often meditate earnestly on the account which they will have to give to God, and that they will be guilty in His sight of the ignorance of the children who shall have been under their care, and also of the sins into which this ignorance may have caused them to fall.

"If those to whose charge they were committed have not taken all the pains they ought to save them from this ignorance, there is nothing concerning which Almighty God will take more strict account, or which He will judge more severely."

The same diligent care and thoroughness is required in all that is done in the school, as, for example, in giving a reading-lesson.

"While one reads, all the other children in the class follow the words in their books. The master must watch very carefully to see that all read to themselves, what one is reading aloud, and from time to time he must put some of them on, to read a few words, that he may take them by surprise, and make sure that they are really following the reading."

This may seem absurdly simple; so do many valuable discoveries and inventions of genius, when once they have been made, and adopted into general use; and it must never be forgotten that this method of teaching, that is, giving a lesson to a whole class of children together, *was* De la Salle's invention, and then quite new.

Here are the instructions for a lesson in arithmetic :—

"After the children have done their sums on the paper, instead of correcting them himself, the master will make the children find out their mistakes for themselves, by rational explanation of the processes. He will ask them, for instance, why in addition of money they begin with the lowest coin, and other questions of the same sort, so as to make sure that they have an intelligent understanding of what they do."

When further advanced the boys were to be made first to copy, and then to compose and write out for themselves, all kinds of letters and documents of a business kind, such as bargains and agreements with workmen, bills of goods delivered, receipts, estimates for work to be done, engagements, contracts, bonds, letters of attorney, leases, whether of dwellings or farms, etc.

They were also at the end of the week to write out what they remembered of the instructions they had received on the portion of the catechism which had been their lesson for the week.

It would not be easy to devise a more practically useful kind of education than this. But there was one other branch of educational training to which De la Salle attached so much importance that he required it to be distinctly taught, and himself wrote a manual of it, which was used in all his schools, and three editions of which were printed during his life.

The title of this book is, "Les Regles de la Bienséance, et de la Civilité Chrétienne" ("The Rules of Good Manners, and of Christian Politeness"). How truly Christian is the groundwork and the spirit of the politeness and good manners which he inculcates, appears in the first page of the preface.

"It is a surprising thing that most Christians only think of civility and good breeding as purely human and belonging to this world; they do not lift up their thoughts, and consider them as duties which relate to God, our neighbour, and ourselves. This shows how little real Christianity there is in the world, and how few persons there are who live and behave according to the Spirit of Jesus Christ. And yet this is the only Spirit which ought to underlie all our actions, if they are to be holy and pleasing to God. And it is a duty of which Saint Paul warns us when he tells the first Christians that if they would live in the Spirit of Jesus Christ, they must also walk or conduct themselves after His Spirit.

"As according to the same Apostle there is not one of our actions which may not be holy, so there is not one which should not be done from purely Christian motives. Therefore all our outward actions, to which alone the rules of good breeding can apply, should bear upon them a character of virtue.

"Christian politeness, then, is a proper and well-regulated behaviour, showing itself in our conversation and outward actions, springing from a feeling of modesty, and of respect, goodwill, and kindliness towards others, and suited to the time, and place, and persons with whom we converse."

The counsels to schoolmasters about themselves are those of one who had made full proof of that ministry, and knew by personal experience the trials and temptations which beset their office. He warns them especially against any kind of harshness and severity towards the children, and gives the following instances of ways in which they may err in that direction:—

" 1. When the punishment inflicted is over much, and the yoke laid upon the children too heavy, which is often the case from the master's want of judgment and discretion; for it happens sometimes that the scholars have neither strength of body nor of mind to bear the burdens that are laid upon them.

" 2. When directions or commands are given in an imperious manner or with harsh words, especially if this arises from some movement of impatience or anger in the master.

" 3. When a master hurries a child too much to do a thing which he dislikes, without giving him time to think and collect himself.

" 4. When he insists as strongly about trifles as about things of importance.

" 5. When he condemns a child's actions without giving himself time to listen to his excuses.

" 6. When, not 'considering himself,' he has no sympathy with the infirmities of children, but exaggerates their faults, and when he reproves or punishes, does so as if he was dealing with a senseless machine rather than with a reasonable being."

The rules about punishment are worth noting.

"In order that punishments may be useful to a scholar there must be the following ten conditions:—1. It must be pure and disinterested, that is, there must be in it no feeling of revenge. 2. Charitable, that is, it must be inflicted from a real love for the child. 3. Just. 4. Proportioned to the fault. 5. Moderate. 6. Peaceable, that is, he who inflicts it must not be moved by anger. 7. Prudent. 8. Voluntary on the part of the scholar, that is, understood and accepted by him. 9. Received with respectful submission; and 10. In silence on both sides."

The faults which he would have masters treat with the greatest severity are five, viz.—1. Untruth-

fulness.   2. Quarrelling.   3. Theft.   4. Impurity.
5. Misbehaviour in Church.

Finally, he enumerates the following twelve virtues as necessary to make up the character of a good schoolmaster:—1. Gravity. 2. Silence. 3. Humility. 4. Prudence. 5. Wisdom. 6. Patience. 7. Self-control. 8. Gentleness. 9. Zeal. 10. Watchfulness.   11. Piety.   12. Generosity.

CHAPTER XII.

THE LARGE HOUSE AT VAUGIRARD.

1698-1703.

THE years 1695, 1696, and 1697, which were spent at Vaugirard were years of unusual peace and tranquillity in the troubled life of the founder of the Christian Brothers, and he turned them to account, as we have seen in the last chapters. While he was thus employed, the number of postulants and novices rapidly increased. From all directions young men came to offer themselves for the work, and the demand for schoolmasters was at the time so great, that although he was quite aware that many did not come from the highest motives, or were mistaken as to their powers, yet it was necessary to receive them for a time, and give them a trial, lest any possible candidate should be lost.

But the house at Vaugirard was not large enough for the increased numbers, and though the distance from Paris was not great, it was sufficient to be an inconvenience. Between it and Paris, a good deal nearer to the city, there was a large block of buildings, which had once been a convent; the Community had been dissolved, and the house stood empty and deserted. It was said to be haunted by ghosts, and this report prevented its being let. De la Salle looked at it; it was just suited for his purpose, and the proprietor was willing to let it to him at a rent of 1600 livres a year—a very low rent for the size of the building and extent of the premises, but nevertheless a considerable sum for one who had nothing. However, he decided to take it, and as by placing his Community there, he would bring it again within the bounds of the parish of Saint Sulpice, he went first to call on the Incumbent to tell him of his purpose.

His old friend M. de la Barmondière had died, and M. de la Chetardie was now Curé, an able, learned, and good man, who had considerable influence both with the Archbishop of Paris, and also with Louis XIV. The king was much attached to him, and was very desirous to make him Bishop of Poitiers; but he always refused to leave his parish. "I have sixty-six reasons," he said, "for not accepting your Majesty's offer." "What are they?" asked the king. "My sixty-six years." He used all his influence to forward good works; his charity to the poor was unbounded; from the day that he was appointed to the cure of Saint Sulpice, he set aside all his income for charity, reserving only so much as was absolutely necessary for his own support and that of one servant.

Such a man was sure to be favourably disposed towards De la Salle and his work. He was at first rather surprised to hear of his intention to hire a house at a rent of 1600 livres a year, knowing that he had a household of about sixty persons to keep, and had nothing to depend on for their maintenance except the good Providence of God. But when he had heard his reasons for doing so, he entirely approved of the step, and promised to contribute fifty livres a year towards the expense. Thus encouraged, De la Salle signed the lease, and moved his Community into the house in April, 1698.

It was unfurnished, but there was then living in the parish a wealthy lady, Madame Voisin, widow of a late Secretary of State, who was noted for the abundance of her alms. At a hint from the curé, the Christian Brothers applied to her, and she gave them seven thousand livres, which enabled them to get the necessary furniture. Having been a convent, the house was provided with a chapel which only needed enlarging. They added a chancel, and dedicated it to Saint Cassianus, the Christian schoolmaster who was martyred by his heathen scholars in the fourth century, a fitting patronage for those who had no prospect indeed of martyrdom at the hands of their scholars, but whose life was spent, and health and strength often sacrificed, in teaching them the faith and the law of God.

As soon as they were well settled in their large house, De la Salle set about adding to the number of their schools; but first he relieved himself of some of his cares, by appointing one of the Brothers to be Master of the Novices, and making another Superintendent of all the schools in Paris. Unfortunately, he was mistaken in both these men, and we shall see by-and-by what serious trouble they brought upon him; but for the present all seemed to go well, and he was able to give more attention to the general work of his Institute.

He began by opening an additional school in the parish of Saint Sulpice. It had such success that it stirred up afresh the envy of the paid schoolmasters, who seized the furniture of the school, and when De la Salle protested, summoned him and the Brothers before a court of law, where the suit dragged on for months. Their complaint was that the Brothers received children who *could* pay, and who *did* pay for their schooling. This was not true, and as they could not prove it, the case was at last decided against them, and the school was opened again after being closed for eight months. It soon filled to overflowing; there were over four hundred children, and six Brothers were employed in it.

The Curé of Saint Sulpice took great interest in these schools. He used to visit them once a month, examine the children, and distribute prizes. He also made a rule that on the first Saturday of every month all the children from the Christian Brothers' schools in the parish should come in procession to the Church of Saint Sulpice. Contemporary writers say that at this time the Christian Brothers had fourteen schools in their hands, and taught above a thousand children; and the sight of such a number of little ones, who would otherwise have been running wild in the streets, walking two and two in orderly procession to the church, attracted notice, and interested good people in the schools, and so help flowed in. Madame Voisin gave largely to the work, and continued a devoted friend of the Society till her death in 1714.

About this time De la Salle was led to take up quite a new branch of educational work. When James II., King of England, was driven from his throne and country by the revolution of 1688, he took refuge in France; Louis XIV. received him with hospitality, and assigned to him the Castle of Saint Germain for his use, and here the exiled king held his court. Many Roman Catholic gentlemen had followed him to France, and some who remained in their own country sent their sons to his court, to be educated and brought up in the Roman Catholic communion. These were chiefly

Irish. The king consulted the Archbishop of Paris where these lads should be placed, and he in turn referred the question to M. de la Chetardie. The Curé of Saint Sulpice made answer that he knew no one so much to be recommended as an instructor of youth as M. de la Salle. Application was made to him, and the end of it was that fifty young Irish gentlemen were committed to his care. The spacious premises of his large house enabled him to receive them comfortably, and as they required a different kind of education from that which his Brothers were trained to give, he took their instruction into his own hands, with the help of one assistant, and succeeded so well that when after a time King James II. came to visit the school, accompanied by the Archbishop of Paris, he was delighted with all he saw, and expressed to M. de la Salle his gratitude and satisfaction.

Thus he came to be looked upon more and more as an authority in educational questions of all kinds, and though primary education for the children of the poor was ever his chief care, he could not refuse his help and counsel when it was asked for in other cases. Parents who had wilful, unmanageable children used to apply to him, and put them into his hands to be reformed.

One remarkable case was that of a young man of good family, nephew of a Bishop; he was destined to the ecclesiastical state, and had received minor orders and the title of Abbé. But he had no inclination for that profession; he was eighteen years of age, and had been sent to the Priests of the Oratory, in the hope that under their training and influence he might be brought to a better mind and prepared for Holy Orders. But they could do nothing with him; he would break open doors, climb walls, and make his escape from their house, to spend the night in gambling and dissipation. At last in despair, they asked M. de la Salle to receive him, and try what he could do with him.

He did so, and the effect was almost like a miracle. The tone and life of the house seemed to affect him as nothing else had done; the saintly Superior had long talks with him, and under his gentle influence the hard heart broke up its fallow ground; he became most earnest and devout in all the religious exercises of the house, and finally besought M. de la Salle as the greatest favour to allow him to enter the Noviciate. He was too prudent to grant this request; he feared lest this sudden fervour should be but a youthful impulse, a fire soon lighted, and as soon extinguished; besides, he could not consent to admit into his humble Institute, without his parents' consent, a young man for whom his family expected high preferment in the Church. The young Abbé did his best to gain their consent, but in vain. His own mind did not change, no arguments could shake his resolution; his desire, instead of cooling, became more fervent.

Time went on, and as his family, tired of his importunity, had left off answering his letters, at last he took their silence for consent, and with renewed entreaties persuaded the Superior to give him the habit. When he found himself clothed in the poor coarse cassock, with the hob-nailed shoes, and all the livery of poverty, his joy was great, and he exclaimed that he would not change his hat for that of a cardinal.

But his happiness was of short duration—his family heard what had been done, and were indignant; nothing was said for a time, but one day they came suddenly, took him by surprise, carried him off, and placed him in another religious house, where he died two years after.

This is only one instance out of many, of the special gift which De la Salle possessed of touching the hearts of the young, and of the wonderful way in which the Grace of God wrought through him for the conversion of souls.

And yet he seems to have had to bear a more than usual amount of sorrow, from failures, and disappointments — disappointments of the most trying kind, because they were caused by those whom he trusted and loved. More than once it happened that those members of his Community in whom he placed the greatest confidence, and to whom he had intrusted offices of most importance, proved unworthy.

Sometimes the success of their work became a temptation to pride and self-confidence, and a spirit of independence possessed them, and led them to resist the authority of their Superior, and so break their vow of obedience. Or, again, it was against the vow of poverty that the tempter prevailed; they found they could easily make money by their teaching, and so they forsook the Community, and set up schools as a speculation of their own.

These falls were a bitter sorrow to the heart of the holy man, who had laboured so earnestly and at so great self-sacrifice to form in them the true religious spirit, while he trained them for their special work. He grieved as a father over the sons whom he loved, and as a founder over the checks and hindrances which such things caused to his work.

One of his most promising undertakings at this time was a Sunday school for lads under twenty years of age, of the artizan and tradesman class, who were at work all the week. His chief object was to keep them from spending their Sundays in objectionable places of amusement, and so he made the school attractive to them, by giving them opportunity not only to improve themselves in reading, writing, and arithmetic, but also to study mechanics, mathematics, drawing, and such things as might be useful to them in the higher branches of their trades and professions. In order to do this efficiently he chose two of the Brothers who had a turn for science and art, and procured for them the necessary instruction. They were put in charge of this higher class of Sunday school, and it soon became very popular. Two hundred lads of all ages under twenty attended it. It began at noon and lasted for two hours; then followed religious instruction, catechism, and an address from one of the Brothers.

Unhappily its great success was too much for the masters who had been specially educated for it. In spite of the most earnest appeals, and solemn warnings from their Superior, they yielded to the temptation, and withdrew from the Society, to set up a paying school on their own account; and as the ordinary training of the Brothers did not fit them for such work, this flourishing school had to be closed, to the great vexation of the Curé of Saint Sulpice, who took much interest and a certain pride in it, as it was the first thing of the kind attempted in France. He would not believe but that it might have been carried on, if M. de la Salle had really wished to do so. He even went so far as to accuse the holy man of falsehood when he told him that he had no master competent to carry on the school. De la

Salle's way of receiving this affront was very characteristic; he was not in the least discomposed by it, no shade of offended pride clouded even for a moment the habitual serenity of his countenance. He only said, "And yet, Monsieur, it is with this lie in my mouth that I am going to say Mass," and went at once to the Church and to the Altar.

After a time another Brother was trained for it, and the school was soon as flourishing as before, and an instrument of great good to the young men of the class for whom it was intended.

Another and much more serious trouble arose out of the conduct of the Brother to whom he had assigned the important office of Master of the Novices. His fault was that of a hard, severe disposition and violent temper. De la Salle was not aware of it, or he would certainly not have placed him over the young Novices; he restrained himself in the presence of the Superior, but while he was absent about affairs of the Community, he treated some of the young men with so much harshness, that without waiting for the return of their Superior, they went to the Curé of Saint Sulpice, to complain of the treatment which they had received.

M. de la Chétardie had been, as we have seen, very favourably disposed towards De la Salle; but the episode of the Sunday school, and some other differences which had arisen between them, had somewhat lessened his regard, and he was too ready to believe that the system which he had established in his Community was unduly severe, and that he was answerable for the treatment of the Novices, whose complaints really were well-founded. On being appealed to a second time by a young master who had been severely punished by the Brother Superintendent of the schools in Paris, he quite made up his mind that this was the case; and without saying anything to the Superior, he took down the depositions, on oath, of the Novices, and sent them with a note of his own to the Archbishop, requesting that there might be an official inquiry into the affair.

The Cardinal de Noailles, who was then Archbishop of Paris, had hitherto shown himself particularly favourable to the Institute of the Christian Brothers, and to their venerable founder; but he was a weak man, easily led by those about him, and when the Curé of Saint Sulpice, in whom he placed unlimited confidence, brought such a charge, he yielded at once, and desired one of his Grand Vicars, M. Pirot, to investigate the matter.

De la Salle was still absent; he had gone to open a school at Troyes. When he returned to Paris the inquiry was going on; but as his manner was, he asked no questions, did not want to hear anything about it, took no steps to defend himself, but waited patiently the good pleasure of Providence.

The Grand Vicar's inquiries resulted in nothing that could be construed as unfavourable to the Superior. All the Brothers expressed themselves as tenderly attached to him, and perfectly satisfied with his government and with their rule ; they only complained of the harshness of those *from amongst themselves*, whom he had set over them. Notwithstanding this, M. Pirot, influenced probably by others who had some grudge against De la Salle, and perhaps not able to understand his silence and the absence of all attempt at self-defence, so reported the case to the Archbishop as to make it appear that De la Salle was in fault ; and when, shortly after, the Superior of the Christian Brothers waited upon the Archbishop, he received him, indeed, with his usual politeness, but after a few minutes' conversation, without any reproof or explanation, said to him, " Monsieur, you are no longer Superior of your Community ; I have provided another."

The words must have fallen like a thunderbolt on De la Salle, who was wholly unprepared for such a sentence. He made no answer, he asked for no explanation, but withdrew in silence, inwardly thanking God for this humiliation, and that, through it, he was at last relieved of the burden which he had so long wished to lay down.

He went home, and said nothing to the Brethren of what had passed. Before long he received a private notice from M. Pirot, that on a certain day, by the Archbishop's command, he would come to instal the new Superior. Fearing that some resistance might be made by the Brothers, he did not tell them what was coming, only gave notice of a general assembly of the Community.

Advent Sunday was the day appointed. All the Brothers who were within reach were assembled in the house. The hall had been prepared and decorated as for a festival. The Brothers were in a state of expectation, not knowing who was coming, or what was going to happen. The Superior, cheerful and serene as usual, superintended the arrangements. Vespers were just over, when a carriage drove up, and the Grand Vicar, M. Pirot, entered the hall, accompanied by a young ecclesiastic who was unknown to them. The stranger was received with great deference by M. de la Salle, and by him conducted to the seat of honour prepared for him; the Grand Vicar sat down beside him, and a bell was rung to summon the whole household. When all were assembled, M. Pirot addressed them. He began by praising their Superior as a man chosen of God to found a great work, and to conduct it to the point which it had reached; he spoke of his virtues, his labours and sacrifices, and was not sparing in his eulogy. The Brethren listened with delight, and their murmurs of approbation at times almost drowned

M. Pirot's voice. But when he turned from M. de la Salle to the young priest whom he had brought with him, and began to extol his merits, and to exhort the Brothers to yield to him, for the future, their obedience in all things, they were at first bewildered, then dumb with astonishment, hardly able to believe their ears ; at last the truth dawned upon them that they were being introduced to a new Superior, and asked to transfer their allegiance from their own Father to him, and they could refrain no longer. One of the principal of them advanced respectfully towards the Grand Vicar, and in the name of all the rest, told him that they had got a Superior, and must request him not to propose to them another.

M. Pirot took no notice of the interruption, motioned him back with his hand, and went on to say that he brought them an official command from the Archbishop, and that it was their duty to obey.

This only added to the tumult. With one voice all, whether Brothers or Novices, cried out together, " Monsieur de la Salle is our only Superior ; we will have no other." They went on to say that the Archbishop must have been deceived, or he never would have done anything so unjust, and so repugnant to the whole Community.

Greatly distressed, De la Salle next addressed them himself. He reminded them of their vow of obedience, and required them, by virtue of his authority as Superior, to submit to the commands of the Archbishop, and not set an example of insubordination and revolt.

His words had no effect; they only repeated their determination to have no other Superior. He had originated their Society and their work, he had conducted it so far, what proof could be alleged that he was no longer fit to guide them? The only purpose of changing their Superior was to change their Rule; and they did not want it changed; they loved it; it was cruel thus to upset the work to which they had wholly devoted themselves.

It might have occurred to the Grand Vicar that such an exhibition of feeling on the part of the Community was in itself an amply sufficient refutation of the charges made against the Superior of harsh and tyrannical behaviour, and if he had been wise, he would have withdrawn from the contest with the best grace he could.

But his pride was touched by their determined resistance to his authority, and he would not yield. He held up the decree of the Archbishop's court, signed and sealed, in which the complaints laid against their Superior were rehearsed, and read it through to them. This only made matters worse; the Brothers could not contain their indignation, and they appealed from the Archbishop misinformed, to the Archbishop better informed.

One of those not least to be pitied during these proceedings was the young Abbé Bricot, who had come there expecting to be solemnly installed as Superior. His position was certainly a painful one, and he did his best to put an end to the scene, by requesting M. Pirot to allow the Community to retain the Superior to whom they were so deeply attached; adding that for his part he could never consent to fill that office in a house, where, although he might be put in possession of the keys, the hearts were closed against him.

But the person who suffered most was De la Salle himself. He was deeply pained at the breach of discipline and obedience, and also he saw his own hope of a life of retirement and prayer once more vanishing away. He did not, however, despair of bringing the Brothers to submit, and as he conducted M. Pirot to his carriage, he said something of the kind to him. The Brothers overheard it, and they would not let it pass; they renewed their declaration that they would have no Superior but their own Father. "If another is forced upon us," they added, "he must bring his Community with him, for we shall leave the house."

The Grand Vicar departed, quite convinced that any attempt to impose another Superior would only lead to the dissolution of the Society, and the overthrow of their work. He reported the state of things to the Archbishop, and added, that if the same feeling existed in other Communites, a religious house would be a Paradise upon earth.

The Archbishop was naturally much vexed. He was angry with his Grand Vicar for having mismanaged the affair; he was angry with the Christian Brothers for their resistance to his authority; and he was angry with De la Salle himself as the cause of it all. Not that he could be accused of insubordination; in his great trouble at what had taken place, he went to the Archbishop, threw himself at his feet, and with tears implored forgiveness for the disobedience of his Community. Sad to say, the Archbishop turned away, and left him without a word. De la Salle meekly accepted this new indignity, and went home to resume his daily life and duties.

Things could not remain in such an uncomfortable kind of dead-lock. The Brothers had recourse to M. de la Chétardie, and he put this very delicate affair into the hands of one of the Priests of Saint Sulpice, a man of tact and discretion, who succeeded in bringing about a sort of accommodation or compromise, after this manner:—Certain members of the Community waited upon M. Pirot to apologize for their behaviour and express their willingness to acknowledge the new Superior, *on condition* that he should be titular Superior only; that he should never come to the house; that nothing should be changed; and that M. de la Salle should retain all his powers.

This was agreed to; the Abbé Bricot came and preached, and then the Te Deum was sung in the chapel. After three months he put in an appearance again, but was seen there no more, and the Archbishop found another post for him.

Peace was thus restored, and to avoid the danger of future complaints, De la Salle took the advice of his ecclesiastical Superiors, and abated something of the strictness of the Rule.

CHAPTER XIII.

PERSECUTION.

1703–1708.

IN the summer of 1703, very soon after the events recorded in the last chapter, the Community of the Christian Brothers were obliged to leave the large house at Vaugirard, which suited them so well. The owner sold it. If M. de la Salle could have bought it he would have done so, but he had not the means, and the new proprietor, wishing to turn it to some other use, gave him notice to quit. With some difficulty, he found a less commodious, but sufficiently large house in the Faubourg Saint Antoine, and thither he moved, after first asking permission of the Curé of Saint Paul, in whose parish it was.

As usual, the change of residence supplied a new field for the labours of the Brothers. Schools were opened in the parish of Saint Paul, as before in that of Saint Sulpice, and a Sunday school was started similar to that which was described in the last chapter.

This was the signal for a fierce attack upon him by the two rival corporations, the schoolmasters and the writing-masters, whose jealousies of one another and long-standing strife have been described in Chapter VIII. They forgot their old enmities to make common cause against the Christian Brothers.

It was not unnatural that they should take alarm at the way in which the education of almost all classes was gradually falling into the hands of the Brothers; and though their schools were still absolutely free, they certainly had assumed a very different character from the poor little charity schools which had been judged not to interfere at all with other educational establishments, or encroach upon their rights. This was the ground of their assault, and a most determined one it was. Both corporations attacked them simultaneously, and De la Salle, who hated law suits, found himself dragged at the same time before the tribunals of the Church and the State. The ordinary schoolmasters were, it will be remembered, under the supervision and protection of the Precentor, who represented the Cathedral Chapter, which in its turn represented the Church, so that their appeal was to the Church Courts. The writing-masters had all along looked to the secular power for support and defence. It was the municipality of Paris which took their side in their long quarrel with the schoolmasters, consequently their appeal was to the police courts.

It would be wearisome to tell of all the moves in this cruel onslaught upon men who, from no motives of earthly interest or worldly gains, were spending their whole lives in doing good. It may suffice to say that for the time their enemies prevailed against them. Not content with attacking them in their work, closing their schools, seizing and confiscating their books and furniture, and imposing upon them heavy fines, they at last procured a sentence against them forbidding them to live together in Paris or to form a Community there, until they should have obtained permission by letters patent from the king.

This sentence was executed with the utmost rigour. It was placarded about Paris; sergeants of police appeared before the house which they occupied in the Faubourg Saint Antoine, with carts, ladders, axes, and hammers; the title over the door, "Les Frères des Écoles Chrétiennes," was torn down; the seats, the tables, the books, everything was carried off; the house was ransacked, pillaged, and left empty and desolate.

De la Salle found a temporary refuge for himself and his Novices in the parish of Saint Roch, and made one last attempt to defend himself and his

Community from these bitter attacks by an appeal to the Parliament. The Parliament had before now taken up the cause of free schools, and there was reason to hope that the highest tribunal in the land, being removed from all petty local jealousies would do justice. This hope, too, was disappointed. The Parliament confirmed the sentence,* and De la Salle was forbidden to open any school throughout the whole extent of Paris or its suburbs without having a formal permission granted, and a definite district assigned by the Precentor. He was condemned, not only as a teacher of schools, but as the founder of a Community for that express purpose, and was forbidden to establish or maintain any Society of the kind in Paris for the future.

Thus was he relentlessly pursued and persecuted on all sides. Church courts and State courts combined to condemn him, and Parliament ratified their sentence. Those who were at bitter enmity between themselves were made friends together in order to attack him. He had not one friend, not

---

* Archives Nationales, L. 492. "Arrêt de la Cour du Parlement du 5 Février, 1706 : Obtenu à la diligence des maîtres et communauté des petites écoles de cette ville, fauxbourgs et banlieue de Paris.

"Contre maistre Jean Baptiste de la Salle, prestre, docteur en théologie, cy-devant chanoine de la cathédrale de Reims, soy-disant superieur des pretendus Frères des Écoles Chrétiennes.

"Et encore contre les nommés Jean Ponce, Joseph et autres tenant école sous les auspices dudit sieur de la Salle en differents quartiers de cette dite ville et fauxbourgs de Paris, sans aucun droit ni qualité," etc.

one protector, not one just and impartial judge. And Paris, to whose benefit he had devoted himself, refused his services, drove him from her, and, after fifteen years of persecution, forced him to transport his Institute elsewhere. He had already done so; six months before he had moved all the Novices, and whatever remained to him of furniture and household goods, to Saint Yon, close to Rouen, where he had found friends and protectors, and a hearty welcome.

But though the mother house and the home of the Novices were no longer in Paris, their schools had not all been suppressed. Those in the parish of Saint Sulpice were still carried on under the sanction and protection of the Curé, and the Brothers in charge of them had to bear the brunt of all the annoyances and persecutions which their enemies could heap upon them. They were determined to drive them away by sheer worry if they could not by actual force; at all hours they would suddenly enter the schools, frighten the children, threaten the masters with law suits, fines, confiscation of goods, and the poor Brothers had no peace, and lived in constant alarm.

Hearing of their troubles and continued persecutions, the Superior came back to Paris. To add to his troubles, he was suffering from a formation in the knee, said to be caused by incessant kneeling and which required a painful operation. It had been performed at Rouen, but badly, and it had to be repeated in Paris. De la Salle underwent it with the calmness and courage which might be looked for in one so inured to mortification and hardness. It is said that during the whole time of the operation he was engaged in saying his office, and that the acutest pain hardly seemed to cause him any distraction, much less did it draw from him any complaint or expression of distress.

At last the persecution became so bitter, that the Brothers were unable to endure it any longer, and the Superior gave them leave to retire from the field. Next day the schools were closed; when the children came at the usual hour they found the doors locked. At first they supposed it was a holiday, but soon it was noised about that the Brothers were gone. When some days had passed, and nothing was heard of them, the parents became alarmed. They went to M. de la Chétardie, and told him that they desired a Christian education for their children, that they were too poor to pay for their schooling, and if the Christian Brothers' schools were closed, their poor children would have no education at all.

The Curé of Saint Sulpice felt the force of their appeal; but he could not expect the Brothers to keep the schools under the perpetual annoyances to which of late they had been subjected. He therefore sent for the opposing faction, and told them that it was he who had invited the Brothers into his parish, that he had put the schools under their charge, that they were supported at his expense, and that he intended, by virtue of his rights as Incumbent, to maintain them in the posts to which he had appointed them.

A legal declaration to this effect was drawn up by two notaries in the presence of the writing-masters themselves, and sent to M. de la Salle as a warrant for the return of the Christian Brothers, and to serve as their protection for the future.

After an interval of three weeks the schools were opened again. But the truce proved a very hollow one; the annoyances were renewed, the children were frightened, the Brothers were worried and disheartened. Once more their Superior withdrew them. The Curé tried to get masters elsewhere, but could not succeed. After repeated attempts, he applied again to M. de la Salle, to send the Christian Brothers back into the parish. De la Salle had no feeling of rancour or ill-will towards him; he was quite willing to let them return if he could have some sufficient guarantee that they would be suffered to do their work without molestation. As the pretext for attacking them was that they received children whose parents could pay, M. de la Chétardie had a list made of all the children, their ages, abodes, and the condition of their parents; and it was arranged that henceforth no child should be admitted into the schools without a ticket from one of the clergy certifying that it was a proper case.

Thus all cause of complaint was removed; the responsibility rested on the clergy, and the Brothers were able to pursue their work in peace.

While this persecution was going on, the work was gradually extending itself through the length and breadth of the land. It seemed as if some fresh ground was occupied, some new foundation made contemporaneously with each hostile attack. Each of these foundations, whereby France was being gradually covered with a net-work of Christian education, had its own peculiar circumstances, its helps, its difficulties, its local interests, its opposers and its supporters; but the method pursued was in the main the same. As the schools were to be entirely free, the first step was to provide the small amount required for the bare necessaries of life for the masters, and the needful outlay in books and school materials. Good people who in their charity cared for the education of poor children, generally agreed together to raise a sufficient sum to begin with. Once the school was established, and the good results were seen, gifts flowed in. Sometimes the voluntary subscriptions were superseded by the liberal donation of a capital sum large enough to yield an annual income sufficient for the maintenance of the school. Ten thousand livres at five per cent. gave an income of about twenty pounds and this was considered sufficient for the support of two Brothers and the necessary expenses of a school. The money was generally vested in four or five trustees, who had power to fill up vacancies in their number as they occurred. The town frequently provided a house; if not, the subscribers rented one, till sooner or later some premises were given or bequeathed for the purpose. When this happened, as it often did, the property was vested in the same trustees as the endowment.

The first Bishop who made application to De la Salle for Brothers to open a school in his Episcopal city was the Bishop of Chartres. He had been a fellow-student with him at Saint Sulpice, and had followed with great interest his after life and the history of his Institute. He was much concerned about education, and had written to ask for masters in 1694. At that time the number was small, and De la Salle was obliged to say he had none that he could send. In 1699 the Bishop wrote to him again, moved thereto by a memorial from all the clergy of the town of Chartres. This document is interesting, as showing their earnest and zealous care for the instruction of children. After saying that they had often conferred together as to the cause of the ill behaviour of the youth of both sexes in the town of Chartres, and had come to the conclusion that it was owing to the lack of good schools and careful teaching of the children, and that they felt they must work might and main to secure that there should be masters and mistresses provided in whom full confidence might be placed, and above all that there should be free schools for the children of the very poor,—the memorial goes on :—

"Having heard that there is at Paris a Priest of singular piety, who makes it his business to bring up and train young men for this work, so that they should have all the necessary qualifications for discharging it worthily, and that he is willing to supply such men to places that ask for them, on condition that their maintenance is provided for (which we are assured costs a very small sum), we have felt ourselves obliged, Monseigneur, to have recourse to your Greatness, and very humbly to beseech you to use your influence, and to employ the alms which are at your disposal to procure for this town so efficient a help, to aid in the reformation of the evils of the people."

When the Bishop's second application was received, the Superior assembled the Brothers, communicated it to them, and consulted them as to the answer he should send. They were unanimously in favour of accepting the invitation and opening for new work; they were all willing to go. De la Salle chose six of the most capable, and added a seventh to keep house and manage their affairs; and this little colony was sent forth to the new ground offered to them.

The Bishop of Chartres made himself responsible for all expenses. On the 4th of October he published a "mandement" reminding parents of their duty to see to the education of their children, announcing the provision which was being made for it, and giving notice that the Écoles Chrétiennes would open on the 12th of the same month. They filled immediately, and the establishment of the Christian Brothers at Chartres prospered in all ways.

The Bishop was tenderly careful of the Brothers. He often went to see them, and would inquire if they had all they wanted; he was very watchful to check any tendency to overmuch austerity or bodily mortifications. He used jokingly to say to them, "If you will not fatten your victim for the sacrifice, at least you must nourish it sufficiently and not overload it with exhausting labour and excessive austerity."

Whenever M. de la Salle went to Chartres to visit the Brothers, the Bishop received him with all honour, and invited him to dine with him. Finding that his invitations were always refused, he one day caused the doors of his palace to be locked while De la Salle was with him, so that he found himself a prisoner, and as he could not escape, he submitted with a good grace and dined at the Episcopal table. After dinner the Bishop and his Grand Vicar rallied him on the hardness of his life and the extreme poverty of his clothing. The good man answered simply, and gave his reasons for the Rule he had adopted. But the Bishop could not bear to see him so badly clothed, and presented him with a cloak, which he had had made on purpose of coarse material that he might have no excuse for refusing it. De la Salle accepted it humbly as an alms, and wore it, till one night in Paris, as he was going home late, he met with thieves, who fancied this garment and took possession of it, without much resistance on his part.

Foundations of the Écoles Chrétiennes followed, as has been already said, almost throughout the whole of France—at Calais, where, besides a school for the children of the town, another was established by the king's particular desire, and supplied with the needful funds from his own purse, for the children of sailors; at Troyes, in Languedoc and Provence, at Avignon, at Rome, at Marseilles, at Dijon, at Rouen, at Mende, at Alais, in the Cevennes, where the Bishop was so well pleased with the Christian Brothers, that he did away with all the other schools in the town, and wrote to De la Salle to ask him to send some more masters, in the following terms:—

"We have here, Monsieur, your Brothers as schoolmasters, and we are so well satisfied with them, that I wish we had many more that they might be dispersed among the towns of the Cevennes, and in all the principal places. If I had thirty, I could find plenty of work for them. I have the honour to thank you for those you have already sent, and to ask you for more.

"I do, and I will do, all I can for them. They do infinite good. I will take care to watch over them, and in order to keep up in them the spirit in which you have trained them, I will give them my counsel freely when I see need for it, and, moreover, I will give you an account of them. . . .

"I hope that you will be able to extend to us the help of your dear good Brothers. . . . You may depend upon it I shall spare no pains to assist them, and I shall enter with affectionate interest into all their little concerns under all circumstances. I ask your good prayers, assuring you, Monsieur, that it is in all sincerity and with my whole heart that I am

"Your very humble and very obedient servant,

"F., FIRST BISHOP OF ALAIS."

"28 January, 1708."

Equally earnest had been the application from Grenoble, a few months before. Here it was not the Bishop, but a charitable association of devout lay folk who commissioned one of the clergy to write and ask for masters, which he did on 30th of August, 1707, as follows:—

"When I was at Paris, about fifteen months ago, I had the honour of speaking to you, Monsieur, to know if you could give us two Brothers of your Community, to keep a free school at Grenoble, and you had the goodness to make me hope that you would grant our request. I think that Mgr. the Bishop of Gap, who remained in Paris after me, will probably have said something to you about it. Since that time we have made all necessary arrangements, both for their lodging and their maintenance. Therefore, I beg you now to let us have two as soon as you can, and to let us know about how much it will be needful that we should supply, as well for the expenses of their journey as for their maintenance at Grenoble. We shall draw the necessary money from a fund devoted to works of charity, and we shall consider this as one of the best to which it can be applied. If you will take the trouble to write me what is required for their journey, I will forward it at once to Paris.

"I am, Monsieur, etc., etc."

Similar applications were made, and schools were founded, at Valréas, at Vans, at Versailles, at Moulins, and at Boulogne-sur-Mer. In all parts, from the north to the south, in the remote districts of Provence, as well as in the neighbourhood of the Metropolis, the Christian Brothers were sought for, anxiously expected, enthusiastically welcomed, and as a rule the results of their work more than fulfilled the expectations of those who sent for them. The movement might originate with the parochial clergy, or with the Bishop, or with the civil authorities, or with private individuals; but the mode of proceeding was pretty much the same in all cases, and there does not seem to have been anything deserving of special notice in the case of those towns which have been mentioned, except Rouen, which claims more particular attention as having been the place where De la Salle found a refuge and a welcome when driven from Paris, and to which he removed the Noviciate and the mother house of his Community.

CHAPTER XIV.

ESTABLISHMENT AT ROUEN.

1705–1712.

IT was in the year 1703 that M. de la Salle was invited to Rouen. The education of the children of the poor had been more attended to there than in many towns. Girls' schools were under the charge of religious Communities of women, and for poor boys there were charity schools; while for boys of the middle classes and those who could pay there were schools kept by the writing-masters (Maitres Écrivains) of whom we have already heard so much. The Rouen branch of this Guild or Corporation seems to have been even more exclusive, and more tenacious of their rights, than those at Paris. They claimed a monopoly of all instruction in writing, arithmetic, book-keeping, and singing, whether in schools or in private houses, and so asserted their privileges, that even the clergy were not allowed to do anything that might seem to encroach upon them. Their jealousy of the free schools, and the care they took lest any children who were able to pay should go to them, was so great that at one time no child could be admitted into a charity school who did not wear round his neck or attached to his hat a square piece of parchment, on which was written "Poor, of the town of Rouen." At the time of which we are speaking this offensive badge had been done away with, and in its place every child was required to bring a certificate from the Curé of his parish that he was a proper case for free schooling.

The charity schools were under the management of a sort of charitable committee (Bureau de Bienfaisance), who administered the funds of the charities of the town, whether endowments, gifts, legacies, subscriptions, or collections in the churches. The committee was originally composed of members of the magistracy, the clergy, and the municipality, who met once a week at the hospital to consider cases of distress, make grants, and transact other business. They were only a deliberative body; the execution of their decisions was entrusted to subordinate officials.

But about the middle of the seventeenth century the composition of the committee had been altered; men of property and standing in the town, some of them belonging to the best families of Rouen, gave up all other avocations, and even their homes, and lived in the hospital, amongst the poor, in order to devote themselves entirely to them, and to what might be called the charity organization of the place—thus forming a permanent board of management instead of the weekly committee meeting.

Education was of course one of the subjects to which they had to attend, and they seem to have done their best for it. In the year 1555, during the former system, four houses had been bought, one in each of the four quarters of the town, to serve as a school. An ecclesiastic was placed in each, who for the petty remuneration of lodging and fifty livres, or about two pounds a year, was to undertake the instruction of the children of the poor "in their Christian Faith, and the commandments of the law, in reading, writing, and chiefly in good living." No wonder that after struggling on, after a fashion, for about a century, these schools had gradually died out, so that in 1655 there was but one.

It was not to be supposed that men would be found among the clergy, willing to give up the higher functions of their office to devote themselves to this humble work, and at such a pitiful rate of remuneration.

The committee tried turning the houses into boarding schools; but only a very limited number of children could be received, and the rest ran wild about the streets. They applied to theological students from the Seminary, who had not yet been ordained, to see if any among them would devote themselves for a time to this work, but without success. They sought for ordinary lay schoolmasters, but here, as elsewhere, it was almost impossible to find men who were capable, and at the same time well conducted and trustworthy; those who were appointed were perpetually disappointing them, and the schools were perceptibly dwindling away.

At last they applied to M. de la Salle, and, as usual, they met with a ready response.

The invitation came from one of the clergy, who had been a fellow-student with him at Saint Sulpice, and had watched his course with great interest; but he does not appear to have been personally acquainted with him, as his application was not made directly to him, but through a common friend, M. Chardon. On hearing of it, De la Salle wrote at once:—

"I have learned from M. Chardon this morning, that you have written to him to ask for some of my Brothers, for Rouen, that you wish for two, and want to know what will be required for them. I am very willing to send you two. As to the cost, you know that we are not hard to satisfy, and that we could not send one alone. If you will let me know for what district they are wanted, and how much people are willing to give, you will oblige me much. I think that we shall easily come to an agreement, and that you will be pleased with those whom I shall send.

"I am with all respect, your very humble and obedient servant,

"DE LA SALLE."

Fifty crowns a year was all that was offered. Two masters could not live upon such a pittance, but the parish for which they were wanted was Darnetal, a manufacturing suburb of Rouen, and De la Salle was the more drawn to take up work there, because it was the place where a school had been first established by his relative, Madame de Maillefer, and by his old friend and fellow-worker, M. Nyel, to whose mission to Rheims was really owing the whole upgrowth of the Institute of the Christian Brothers.

He, therefore, consented to send two masters, and the success of the school under them was so great that the Archbishop of Rouen heard of it, and wished to have all the other free schools of the town placed under their care. He had some difficulty in persuading the managers of the charities of Rouen to agree to this, but he succeeded at last, and M. de la Salle was invited to come himself with his Brothers, to take charge of the schools.

He was ready, and set out immediately, travelling on foot with his companions. At night they lodged at any little inn or house of entertainment they could find, and all along they followed the prescribed devotions of their Rule as exactly as if they were at home. People wondered at them as they went, and asked who these men were, so grave and recollected in their demeanour, clothed in such an unusual garb, who walked on in silence, and as soon as they reached an inn, made it their first business to find a quiet room where they might say their prayers.

When they arrived at Rouen, the Charities Committee or Board of Management had changed their minds—they did not wish to have the Christian Brothers. The Archbishop's mind, however, had not changed, and he was a man of mark and power, Monseigneur Colbert, son of the famous Minister of that name. He called a meeting of the committee, and by his influence he brought them round. The Brothers were put in charge of the schools, and before two months had elapsed, more masters were sent for from Paris.

For some time De la Salle had been thinking of moving his Novices from Paris, where the Institute was so incessantly worried and persecuted, and seeking a quieter home for them elsewhere; and when he found how kindly disposed the Archbishop of Rouen was to him and his work, it seemed as if that might be the place for them. He went to the Archbishop and told him what was in his mind, and received the fullest approbation and encouragement, with a promise of help and support.

A little way from the town, at the end of the Faubourg Saint Sever, there was a large and handsome old house, which stood in a walled garden of considerable extent, planted with fine old trees. It was a peaceful place, shut out from the noise and bustle of the town; once within the gates, one could fancy oneself in the country. A former proprietor had built a chapel in the grounds, and had dedicated it to Saint Yon, martyr, and disciple of Saint Denys, and the house took its name from this chapel. At last it had come by inheritance to belong to Madame de Louvois, sister-in-law of the Archbishop of Rheims; she had let it to some Benedictine Nuns, who had enlarged the chapel for their own use. It was exactly what M. de la Salle wanted, and the Nuns were willing to give it up to him. Very secretly, for fear of rousing opposition, he went to Madame de Louvois, who knew all about him through her connection with Rheims, and counted it an honour to further his work in any way. So Saint Yon was let to him for six years, at the almost nominal rent of four hundred livres or sixteen pounds a year. De la Salle took possession of it immediately, moved what furniture he had into it, and established the Novices there, and all those of his Community who were not engaged in schools, in the month of August, 1705, just six months before the decree of the Parliament of Paris ordered their expulsion from that city.

Henceforth Saint Yon became the mother house of the Institute. The Archbishop granted to the

Superior all needful powers and privileges. One of the best and most capable of the Brothers, the Frère Barthelemy, who succeeded M. de la Salle in the office of Superior, was made head of the house and Master of the Novices.

As soon as the move had been accomplished and the necessary arrangements made, De la Salle assembled all the Brothers that he could, for a retreat of eight days, that in the peaceful calm of their new home their fervour might be renewed, and their spirits soothed and tranquillized after the troubles and persecutions which had made their life at Paris of late so unrestful.

As elsewhere, work of various kinds opened before him. Besides being the mother house of the Institute and the home of the Novices, Saint Yon became a boarding school for unmanageable boys, and for those whose parents did not wish to educate them at home, and a reformatory for older and more depraved lads, who were subjected to a strict discipline and careful surveillance, generally with the best effect.

The Committee or Board of Management was hard and parsimonious in its dealings with the Christian Brothers. The grant which was made to them out of the charitable funds at its disposal was quite insufficient for their maintenance, and if it had not been for the charity of individuals and the kindness of the Archbishop, they could not have lived. They were very soon deprived of this last resource. Monseigneur Colbert died in 1707, and his successor Monseigneur d'Aubigné was prejudiced against them, and gave them plainly to understand that they were to expect no help or support from him. This was a great loss, but private beneficence supplied them with the necessaries of life, and though they had nothing more, and often barely so much, they held on bravely till a time of great scarcity came. It was the year 1709; there had been a bad harvest, followed by a long and severe winter, and the scarcity amounted to famine almost all over France.

In this distress, De la Salle called back the Novices to Paris, leaving only a sufficient number of Brothers at Rouen to keep the schools going. He was no better off at Paris, but he felt it safer to have them near him that he might strengthen their faith, and cheer them under their sufferings. He himself never wavered in his trust in Providence, and although the scourge of famine fell heavily upon him, it was never above that he was able to bear. When things were at the worst some relief came.

One day there was no food in the house, no money in the purse, no credit to be had at the baker's. As M. de la Salle was going out to say Mass, he met a charitable person, who asked him where he was going. "I am going to celebrate the holy Mass," he replied, "and to pray God to send what is needful for to-day, to our Community; for we are quite without food, and have no means to get any." "Go in peace," answered the other; "I will see about it myself;" and he went at once to the Brothers' house, and gave them ten crowns, which was sufficient for their immediate needs. In due time the famine abated; a favourable harvest restored plenty to the land, and the pressure of this distress passed away.

But for De la Salle there seemed to be no immunity from troubles, hardly even any interval of rest. The nature of his trials varied, but there was no cessation of them.

That which next followed was more trying to him than the famine had been. That was a dispensation of Providence, and came straight from heaven; this was caused by the treachery of some among his own sons. A plot was laid against him in his own house; it was led by an ambitious Brother who wanted to make himself Superior, and took occasion from the sufferings they had gone through during the time of scarcity, to sow discontent in the hearts of his companions, and to persuade them that the Superior mismanaged the affairs of the Community, and wasted the funds which might have sufficed for their support. For some time their plot was brewing silently, quite unsuspected by the Superior. Outsiders knew of it, and did all they could to promote it. It was brought to light by the confession of one of the Brothers who had been partly won over, and induced to take part in it; but he repented himself in time, and laid bare the whole scheme in full chapter.

The rest were indignant, and urged that the guilty one should be expelled from their Society, and this De la Salle was compelled reluctantly to do, finding it hopeless to win him back by kindness. Peace was thus restored. But other troubles followed—one in particular, which not only defrauded him of the small fund which he had laid by in store for the needs of his poor Community, but cast a grave imputation on his own character.

The blow was dealt by men whom he had trusted, and it renewed in him the feeling he had had before, of being a hindrance and obstacle to the work which he had so much at heart, and for which he had sacrificed all.

He determined to withdraw for a time from public view, in hopes that when he was no longer there to provoke the attacks of his enemies, the Brothers would be left in peace.

He told no one of his intention except the Frère Barthelemy, to whom he privately committed the government of the Community during his absence.

It was a difficult and delicate office to discharge; he was to act as Superior without being really so, and without any formal delegation of authority to him. If this had been done, it would have revealed the intended absence of the Superior, whereas his purpose was to vanish silently from the scene, and leave the Society to go on without him.

Frère Barthelemy was, however, a man of tact and discretion, gentle, and at the same time firm, of deep piety, strict in the observance of the Rule, and much esteemed in the Community; he seemed in all ways fitted for the charge. To him De la Salle confided his plans, and gave him such instructions as he could for the guidance of the Institute during his absence. This done, he left Paris in the Spring of 1712.

CHAPTER XV.

TRAVELS IN THE SOUTH.

1712–1714.

DE LA SALLE'S object in thus withdrawing from public observation was to promote the peace and well-being of his Institute, not to seek rest for himself. The yearning desire of his heart for retirement was as strong as ever, but he felt that it was not the will of God for him, at least not yet. He therefore turned his steps towards the south of France, that he might employ the time of his absence in visiting the numerous establishments of his Community which had been made in those Provinces, and which he had not yet seen.

His journeys, as we know, were always made on foot; and we may picture him to ourselves like those first sent forth by his and their Lord and Master, as taking "nothing for his journey save a staff only; no scrip, no bread, no money in his purse." But, unlike them, who were sent by two and two, he was alone; and as he set forth in his poverty and loneliness to travel thus from Paris to Avignon, he might almost have taken up the words of the great Apostle, and said of himself, "In journeyings often, in perils of waters, in perils of robbers, in perils by my own countrymen, ... in perils in the city, in perils in the wilderness, ... in perils among false brethren; in weariness and painfulness, in watchings often, in hunger and thirst, in fastings often, in cold and nakedness. Beside those things that are without, that which cometh upon me daily, the care of all the Churches." *

Like Saint Paul, his journey was not without comfort also; he was welcomed with reverent delight by the faithful Brethren, to whom the sight of his face was a joy and consolation.

Thus it was at Avignon, where he arrived at the end of Lent. It had been the first foundation in the south, and the Brothers had been working there for ten years without seeing him. They rejoiced to have him with them, they clung to him, told him all their troubles, hung upon his words, and would fain have kept him with them, not only for their own comfort, but because they dreaded the perils of his journey through the wild and mountainous district of the Cévennes, which was infested by robbers.

* 2 Cor. xi. 26–28.

He left them, however, and reached Alais in safety, where the Bishop, who had written so earnestly to ask for Brothers, received him with every token of respect, and expressed his full satisfaction in them and their work. The same kind of reception greeted him at all the places which he visited on his way to Marseilles, and in that city it was unusually cordial; clergy and laity alike hastened to welcome him, and to express their readiness to further his work in every possible way.

There was already a flourishing school under the charge of his Brothers, and money was offered to found another. The proposal came to nothing through the want of hearty co-operation on the part of the Curé of the parish where the school was to be. He could not help reverencing De la Salle, but he had no real sympathy with him. He felt the austerity of his life to be a silent rebuke to worldly-minded clergy; and, besides, he wanted to have the school under one or more ecclesiastics, who could occasionally help him in his parish work. With this design he went to the donors of the money, and persuaded them to devote their charity to something else. This was a disappointment; but when friends came with long faces to condole with De la Salle on the failure of his plans, he received them with a bright smile, and simply said, "God be praised; it appears that it is not His will that we should have another school here at present."

The disappointment did not deter him from entertaining a much larger and more important design, viz. to found a home for Novices at Marseille. Many things made this desirable. The patois of the southern provinces was in fact a different language from the French of the north, and it was necessary that schoolmasters for this part of France should be natives of the country, and familiar with the dialect. Paris and Saint Yon were too far off to send young men to for their training; neither could those houses, on account of the distance, be used as homes of rest, or of retreat, for the Brothers already at work in the south; and we know that De la Salle considered an annual retreat as essential to the spiritual life of the members of the Institute.

These and other reasons induced him to mention the subject to those who had expressed so much willingness to help him, and it was warmly taken up; every one saw the advantage of it, and all were anxious to help in carrying it out. Funds were soon collected; a suitable house was found, hired, and furnished; Novices presented themselves; and the whole thing was in operation by the month of September, 1712. The clergy of the town appeared to take a great interest in it, and the Bishop took it under his special protection.

De la Salle accepted all this help and favour thankfully, but not without grave misgivings; it was altogether unlike his former experiences, and he doubted how far it was real and to be trusted. Before very long his suspicions proved to be well founded. There was at that time a strong Jansenist party among the clergy at Marseille, and they hoped by a show of marked cordiality, and by taking up his work with great zeal, to win the Superior of the Christian Brothers over to their side in the strife which was then disturbing the peace of the Church in France. When they found that they could not do so they turned against him; withdrew all the support they had promised, persuaded the Novices that the Rule was too severe, tampered with the professed Brothers, circulated slanderous reports against him, and so thwarted and opposed him that he felt his work there was for the time at an 'end. He left the place and withdrew to Grenoble. On his way there he stopped at Mende, where there was an establishment of his Community, and where he had been welcomed with every demonstration of affection a few weeks before. But everything was changed; the calumnies of his enemies had been so industriously circulated, that they had reached outlying stations, and when, weary and footsore, after a pilgrimage of forty-six leagues, he knocked at the door of the Christian Brothers' house, he was refused entrance, and was obliged to ask at a Convent of Capuchins that hospitality which was denied him by his own children.

At Grenoble he found faithful sons and a loving welcome. He remained with them about six months, spending almost all his time in private prayer and the devotional exercises of the Community.

He chose a little cell at the top of the house, where unseen, and as far as possible forgotten by man, he could pour out his heart to the only Friend that never failed him, and seek strength and guidance for the future.

It was a time of great peace, only interrupted by occasional absences, as when he went for a few days to the Grande Chartreuse, to visit the wonderful foundation of his great predecessor Saint Bruno, like himself a Canon of Rheims, who had resigned his Canonry, to obey the call to a higher life of austere monasticism, and had selected for his convent a spot where the rugged and sublime majesty of nature accorded well with the severity of his rule, and the life of silence and contemplation to which it bound his followers.

It was the month of January, 1714, that De la Salle visited the Grande Chartreuse, so that he must have seen it in all the stern beauty of its winter snows, and experienced the full rigour of the life in those unwarmed stone cells. It is not surprising to find that shortly after his return to Grenoble he was attacked by acute rheumatism, apparently rheumatic fever. After long and intense suffering, it was treated, according to the barbarous medical practice of the period, by a process as near broiling as the human body could endure, stretched naked over a hot fire on a sort of gridiron. This torture, which was repeated for several days, gave relief to the pains of rheumatism, but left him very weak. As soon as he had recovered strength enough to walk, he accepted the invitation of a friend, the Abbé Saléon, to spend a fortnight in his house at Parmenie for rest and change of air.

Parmenie was a steep and isolated hill about seven leagues north-west of Grenoble, with a beautifully wooded table land on the top, which commanded a splendid view over the rich and fertile valley of Grésivandan, the Isère, and many towns and villages at its foot. It was a place of pilgrimage, with a hermitage, near which was the house and property of his friend. Here De la Salle spent a restful fortnight, and here he made the acquaintance of M. Dulac de Montisambert, a young man of noble birth, who had been brought up religiously in the fear of God. He had entered the army very young, and was a lieutenant at fourteen. During the time of his military service he had fallen among bad companions, and had been led into gambling and other evil ways. At the battle of Malplaquet he was dangerously wounded; a ball passed right through his body, and he was brought face to face with death. In this danger, by the Grace of God, he "came to himself." He recovered from his wound, and remained some time in the regiment, leading an irreproachable and religious life, and edifying all his comrades as well as his superior officers by his good example.

When he was twenty-two he resolved to give himself up entirely to the service of God, but without any distinct idea, how, or where, or in what kind of life. Fearing opposition, he said nothing of his intentions, but left the regiment secretly, sold his horse, and came to Grenoble, where he spent about ten months nursing the sick in hospitals, praying in the churches, and trying to learn something of the life (so new to him) to which he wished to devote himself. At the end of this time, he applied to the Capuchins at Grenoble, and asked to be received as a lay-brother in their convent. They asked for his baptismal register and the consent of his parents. The latter he had no hope of obtaining, and to have taken steps to procure the former would have revealed to his friends where he was. As he could not produce either, he was refused admission. He next knocked at the door of the Grande Chartreuse. But the Cistercians also feared that it would bring trouble upon them if they received him without the sanction of his family ; so they refused him, on the ground that, not having learned Latin, he could not say the Breviary.

He then made a pilgrimage to Italy, visited many sacred places on foot, leading a life of great hardship, and returned to Grenoble more eager than before to enter a religious Community. He sought admission to another house of the Cistercian order, but was again refused, not, however, on the same grounds as before. The Abbot told him that he could not receive him, because he was persuaded that God was calling him elsewhere. After this he retired to the Hermitage of Parmenie, and was there in retreat, when De la Salle came to the house of M. Saléon. The Chaplain of the Hermitage, who heard the young man's confessions, and knew of his difficulties, introduced him to M. de la Salle as one who might perhaps be a fit subject for his Institute. De la Salle was at first rather shy of the young officer, and feared that he could hardly submit himself to the Rule and work of his humble Community. But Dulac threw himself on his knees before him, told him the earnest desire of his heart to join some religious Order, a desire which was only deepened by the refusals he had met with, and implored him to allow him to enter his Society. His earnestness and evident sincerity prevailed. De la Salle accepted him as a Novice. He received the name of Irenæus, and after going through the exercises of the Noviciate at Grenoble, he was sent to take charge of a school at Avignon, thence to Paris and to Saint Yon, where he was made Master of the Novices, and Assistant-Superior.

De la Salle returned to Grenoble in time to keep the Festival of Saint Joseph (March 19), the Patron Saint of his Community, with the Brothers there; and it may probably have been three or four weeks later that he received a letter from the Brothers in Paris, summoning him to return in the following terms :—

"Monsieur our dear Father,—
"We, principal Brothers of the Écoles Chrétiennes, having in view the greater glory of God, the greater good of the Church and of our Society, are convinced that it is of extreme importance that you should resume the care and the general conduct of the holy work of God, which is also yours, since it has pleased the Lord to employ you in founding it, and guiding it for so long a time. Every one is persuaded that God has given, and still gives you, the graces and talents needful for rightly governing this new Society, which is so useful to the Church; and we can in all sincerity bear witness that you have always ruled it with great success and edification. It is for this reason, Monsieur, that we very humbly entreat you, and in the name and on behalf of the Society in its corporate capacity, to which you have promised obedience, we command you to take up again immediately the charge of the general government of our Society. And we are, with the deepest respect, Monsieur our dear Father, your very humble and very obedient inferiors.
"In faith of which we have signed.
"Done at Paris, the 1st April, 1714."

In order to understand the cause of this strangely peremptory communication, it will be necessary to inquire what had been taking place at Paris during the long absence of the Superior.

CHAPTER XVI.

TROUBLES DURING HIS ABSENCE, HIS RETURN, AND ELECTION OF A NEW SUPERIOR.

1714–1717.

FRÈRE BARTHELEMY, who had been left in charge during the absence of the Superior, had a certain authority as Master of the Novices; but his powers were vague and undefined, and in no degree supplied the want of the strong hand which had hitherto held the reins, and guided the Community with fatherly love, but with the firmness which comes from a clear intuition and definiteness of purpose, coupled with a consciousness of rightful authority.

There had long been a desire on the part of the parochial clergy in Paris, and others, to effect a change in the constitution of the Society. They valued the Christian Brothers and their work; in fact, as we have already seen, the difficulty of finding good schoolmasters was so great that they would have been much at a loss to carry on the schools without them; but at the same time they winced under the consciousness of being thus beholden to men who looked to another authority than theirs, who belonged to a new and obscure Order, followed their own rules and methods, and were only laymen, for the most part of humble birth and little education beyond what their profession required.

They wanted to do away with the central unity of the Society, and to give it more of a Diocesan, or at least a local character, with separate branch houses, each independent of the rest, having its own band of Brothers, and its own small Noviciate to keep up the supply. The Brothers of each house to be permanently attached to it, not removable, and to be under the control of the clergy, with an Ecclesiastical Superior not chosen out of the Community.

From a parochial point of view there was much to be said for this scheme, but it was not the idea which the founder had conceived and to the realization of which all his plans had been directed. His conception was strictly that of one single family, under one fatherly head, with one paternal home, and one rule which should be law to all alike. However widely the Community might spread throughout France, or even beyond it, this unity was to be an essential element of their constitution. Wherever the Brothers might be called to exercise their functions, their duties were the same; they ought therefore, he conceived, to be formed after the same manner, to receive the same training, to cultivate the same virtues, to be imbued with the same spirit, and as far as possible to be fashioned on the same model. In order to effect this unity of character, it was requisite that they should all pass through the Noviciate, not only spending a year at least there at first, but returning there from time to time to be remoulded, as it were, after their true pattern, and, like tools which have become blunted by use, to be reset and polished, and sent back to their work with keen and newly sharpened edge.

Besides this frequent return to the mother house, the Brothers wrote to the Superior once a month, and he to them. He also visited them occasionally. Thus the connection between them, begun in the Noviciate, was kept up; the Superior was *en rapport* with all the Brothers, wherever they might be stationed, and could check any irregularity at once. If any one showed symptoms of slackness or laxity in the observance of the Rule, he could be at once recalled, or moved from the surroundings which were of a disturbing nature to some other place. In order to carry out this system, it was necessary that the Superior should be invested with supreme powers.

At the same time there was no lack of deference to Ecclesiastical authority. No school was ever opened without the consent of the Bishop of the Diocese, and wherever they worked the Brothers looked to the clergy of the parish, for counsel and support, and pressed them constantly to visit the schools; but in the management of the schools, as well as in the ordering of their own lives, they were bound to adhere strictly to their Rule. This was plainly necessary. If the clergy had been allowed to interfere and make alterations in these respects, the unity of their system would soon have been destroyed. What was approved of in one Diocese or parish might have been objected to in another, and confusion would have been sure to ensue.

With a keen perception of these almost certain consequences, De la Salle had always resolutely adhered to his own original idea; his refusal to modify it was probably the occasion of the coolness which existed, during all the latter years of their intercourse, between him and the Curé of Saint Sulpice. As long as he was at Paris nothing could be done by the advocates of the other theory, but during his long absence they thought to take advantage of Frère Barthelemy's undefined position to alter the constitution of the Society according to their own views. They represented to him that it was too much for any man to have the supervision of such a numerous Community, with so many establishments in all parts of France; that even M. de la Salle had broken down under the charge, and had been obliged to withdraw from it; and that he who had neither his learning, nor his age, nor his experience could not be equal to it.

Frère Barthelemy was much too humble to dispute this, but he was faithfully attached to the Rule of his Society, he knew that his authority was only temporary, and he was determined to restore that which had been entrusted to him, unimpaired into his Superior's hands again. He answered that he could not of his own authority alter the constitution of the Institute, that the rules had been accepted by all the Brothers, and that they must be consulted before any change was introduced. But he consented, at their instigation, to write to the Brothers in charge of the different houses, requesting them to choose each for themselves an Ecclesiastical Superior who might direct them during the absence of M. de la Salle, as he himself was not capable of doing so. A few agreed to do this, but the larger number wrote back that they could not take a step so contrary to the constitution of their Society; and some of the clergy themselves declined to accept the office when it was offered to them.

The Archbishop of Paris had nominated a certain Abbé de Brou to be inspector of the schools at

Paris; but when he and M. de la Chétardie laid before him a note of some alterations which they proposed to make in the Society of the Christian Brothers, the Archbishop kept the paper without giving any answer for seven or eight months, and then wrote to the Abbé de Brou that he desired nothing should be changed, adding words expressive of his high esteem for M. de la Salle.

Thus the danger was for the time averted, but the situation was sufficiently critical to make the faithful Brothers, Frère Barthelemy especially, very anxious for the return of the Superior. They wrote more than once entreating him to come back, and receiving no answer, they resolved to send him a formal summons in the name of the whole Community.

This found him at Grenoble, as related in the last chapter, and by his vow, he was bound to obey; so he took leave of his friends and children in that town, and set out for Paris. He made some stay at Lyons, to study the educational work of M. Demia, and took the opportunity to make a kind of Visitation tour amongst the houses of his Community which lay on his way. This delayed his arrival, and it was not till the 10th of August, 1714, that he reached Paris. His first words to the Brothers were, "Well, here I am; what do you want with me?"

They answered by entreating him at once to

resume the direction of the Society. He resisted on many grounds; but they had suffered too much during his absence to be willing to consent to his wish to retire. They fell at his feet and implored him to retain the office and title of Superior, but to delegate the details of administration to Frère Barthelemy, who was now accustomed to them.

De la Salle could not refuse so urgent a request, and had to resign himself to take up the burden once more, but as far as possible he confined himself to the spiritual department of his office, and left the management of the ordinary affairs of the Community to others.

His position was somewhat delicate. The Abbé de Brou, who seems to have been a good man, with no wish to make mischief, had nevertheless, by virtue of the Archbishop's appointment of him as Inspector of Schools, interfered a good deal with the Brothers in their work, and exercised a sort of authority over them; he had even claimed the title of Superior, and taken upon himself to accept or refuse postulants, and at first he was not at all inclined to surrender what he considered his rights. The gentle firmness of M. de la Salle, however, won the day at last, for when, some time after, the Curé of Mende wrote to the Abbé de Brou to ask for some more Brothers, the latter answered him as follows:—

"I have informed M. de la Salle of that which you do me the honour to write about, and he will see to it. He seems to me to be in some difficulty how to find good men for your town, in place of the Brothers who are leaving you. However, he has a great desire to maintain your school, and he intends to provide for it immediately. This is all that I can say to you on the subject, for since he has returned to Paris, I think it is my duty to resign the government of the Society to him, as I only took charge of it during his absence.

"Paris, 5 October, 1714."

The authority of De la Salle was, therefore, at this time quite re-established, and yet we find him in the following year giving up going to Saint Yon, at Rouen, which he wished and intended to do, because the Abbé de Brou disapproved of his doing so, and wished him to remain at Paris. Of course he had no right to forbid him to go, but De la Salle was always more ready to obey than to command; so he yielded at once, and went back to his house.

His presence, however, was really wanted at Saint Yon, and the Brothers knew it; they went to M. de Brou, and represented to him the disadvantage that would result if he continued to oppose his journey to Rouen. The Abbé was amazed at the wonderful submission and obedience of a man so far above him in age, in holiness, and in position and he at once withdrew his objection. De la Salle on hearing this, set out immediately, and arrived at Saint Yon early in December, 1715.

While there he received a visit from two earnestly

religious laymen, M. Gense, of Calais, and M. de la Cocherie, of Boulogne, who had come to Rouen on purpose to make his acquaintance. They were much interested in his work, and made many inquiries about the first beginning of it, and the difficulties which he had had to contend with; and spoke with admiration of the courage with which he had faced his difficulties and triumphed over them. M. de la Salle replied that it was the work of God. Speaking of himself, he said with his usual great simplicity—

"I must tell you that if God, when He showed me the good this Institute might do, had at the same time revealed to me the troubles and the crosses which would go along with it, my courage would have failed, and far from undertaking it, I would not have touched it with the tips of my fingers. I have been exposed to constant opposition, and persecuted by many Prelates, even by some from whom I had hoped for support and help. My own children, those whom I had begotten in Jesus Christ, whom I had cherished with more than ordinary tenderness, and cultivated with special care, and from whom I expected most, have risen against me, and have added to external crosses interior ones, which are far more painful. In a word, if God had not evidently put forth His Hand to uphold this building, it would long ago have been a heap of ruins. The magistrates joined with our enemies and lent their authority to support those who were trying to overthrow us. As our work is specially offensive to the whole class of schoolmasters, we find in each one of them a declared and irreconcilable adversary, and as a united body they have been armed with all the powers of the State for our destruction. And yet, in spite of all their efforts, the building has stood, though often on the point of falling; and this it is which makes me hope that it will yet stand, and that it will at last triumph over all persecutions, and render to the Church the services which she has a right to expect of it."

In these words the venerable man gave indeed a true description of that long sowing in tears which he had gone through, in order that others might reap in joy. To him had been shown the work; his children were to see the glory.

M. Gense pressed him to return his visit, by going to see him at Calais. At first he declined on account of his many occupations, his age, and infirmities; but there were already many schools in the north in charge of members of his Community, and others in prospect, and when Frère Barthelemy represented to him that a visit from him would be very useful to them, he consented to go.

At Calais he was received with great honour by all. M. Gense would fain have had him as his guest, but he chose rather to lodge with the Brothers, who had a house in the town. One day he consented to dine with M. Gense, and this gentleman, who was extremely desirous to have a likeness of him, thought he could manage it by having a portrait-painter unknown to De la Salle in the room, hidden behind a curtain, whence he was to catch such glimpses as he could of his face. This went on with some success for a time; but unfortunately a movement of the artist caught the eye of De la Salle. He detected the plot, and at once rose from table with a displeased look, coldly thanked his host, and left the room. He could not conceive why any one should care to have his portrait, and he felt that an unfair advantage had been taken of him. M. Gense followed him to the house of the Christian Brothers, and tried to persuade him to return, but could not succeed.

From Calais he went to Saint Omer, and from Saint Omer to Boulogne, and thence back to Rouen, where he was laid up for two months with a serious attack of illness. He then resolved no longer to defer his resignation of the Superiorship. He was not very old, only sixty-five, but the fatigues and hardnesses of his life had prematurely aged him; he felt that his death was not far off, and he longed to be free to spend the time that remained to him in prayer. Having laboured for others all his life, it was natural that he should ask for a little time to himself at last, to prepare for that one supreme act of a Christian's life, his death.

The Brothers could no longer raise their former objections. Ever since his return he had left all the practical work in the hands of Frère Barthelemy, though to satisfy them he had consented to retain the title of Superior. The title was all that he had now to divest himself of; but he was very anxious that the election should be regularly and constitutionally made, so as to leave no opening for future disturbance. It was also of consequence that it should be done quietly, so that those who might be inclined to interfere should have no opportunity of doing so.

To this end it was agreed that the Frère Barthelemy should make a tour through all the houses of the Community to inform the Brothers of the state of things, and gain their consent to a change of Superior. This was successfully accomplished. He set out in December, 1716, and returned in March, 1717, having met with cordial consent from all. Whitsuntide was the time fixed for the election, and each establishment of the Christian Brothers was to send a representative to take part in the ceremony.

When the time came there were assembled at Saint Yon representatives from Alais, Boulogne, Calais, Dijon, Grenoble, Guise, Laon, Macon, Marseille, Mende, Moulins, Paris, Rheims, Rouen, Troyes, Versailles, and Saint Denis.

As soon as all had arrived, De la Salle addressed them. He laid before them the reasons which had led him to resign, and why he was so anxious to see a constitutional election made before his death; he explained to them the rules which were to be followed in the election (chiefly borrowed from those of Saint Ignatius), and exhorted them to seek earnestly the guidance of the Holy Spirit in a retreat of two days, which was to be made before the election. He concluded his address with these words:—

"Purify your intentions and your desires, if you would become the organs of the Holy Spirit to name him whom He has chosen. Put away all human sounds, do not listen to the voice of nature, reject all false lights and private prejudices. Act in this choice without interest, without preference, without sympathy and without antipathy, without passion, without inclination, without either natural attraction or repugnance. Keep your hearts in a state of complete indifference, and do not suffer them to incline to any one except to him who shall be found to have the largest number of votes. Since it is not you who are to choose, but God Who chooses in you and by you, lift up your hearts to Him, and never be weary of addressing to Him the prayer of the Apostles, 'Show whom Thou hast chosen.' If you desire to know this, give your vote to him for whom your conscience demands it, to him whose merits point him out, to him whom you would choose if you were at the point of death, to him who is most fit to govern the Institute, who is most filled with its spirit, who is most capable of maintaining its rule, of kindling its fervour, of helping forward your own sanctification. Name him whom you know to be the most enlightened amongst you, the wisest, the most virtuous, the most steadfast. Give your vote to him who possesses in the highest perfection these seven qualities so necessary for one who is to bear rule in the house of God—prudence, gentleness, watchfulness, firmness, piety, zeal, and charity; to him who unites in himself in the greatest degree those virtues which are not commonly found together, zeal and prudence, discernment and charity, firmness and gentleness, kindness and strictness; to him who has sweetness without softness, vigilance without restlessness, firmness without stiffness, zeal without bitterness, kindness without weakness, prudence without insincerity.

"Give your vote to him who is the most saintly, or who desires to become so; who may be to you a pattern to be copied in all things; to him who will be the most humble in the highest place, who will have a Father's heart towards you, and will make you love his authority.

"In making this choice, pay no regard to talents, or birth, or age, or standing in the Community, or outward appearance, or stature. In your Superior you are not to see man, but God. You will be sure to choose him whom God has chosen, if you seek for one who is after His heart, not after your own; a man of grace, and in whom grace works, not a man after your taste, or in whom nature rules."

The Brothers went into retreat on the 6th of May, and on the 8th of May, 1717, the Frère Barthelemy was unanimously elected as the second Superior of their Society.

CHAPTER XVII.

REST.

1717–1719.

AND so at last his heart's desire was granted, and Jean Baptiste de la Salle found himself relieved of the burden which he had borne for so many years, amid so many trials and contradictions, and free to give himself up to that life of uninterrupted communion with God, after which he had always yearned. It must have been a wonderful thing for those members of the Community who had been long under him, and who had known all his work, to see him take his place among them as a simple Brother; and the spirit and manner in which he did so must have had more effect in raising the tone, and deepening the inner life of the Brothers than all his instructions and exhortations, however fervent and often repeated.

Humility and obedience were the two graces which shone out most conspicuously in this great servant of God. In all things he took the lowest place. In the refectory he would sit below the serving brothers, and insisted on being helped last. With difficulty he was persuaded to say grace, on the ground that he was the only Priest in the house. He chose for himself the humblest room, a dark little cell on the ground-floor, down some steps leading to the stables. Here his time was spent in prayer and meditation. He retained, of course, the exercise of his Priestly functions, said Mass, and heard confessions, and in spiritual matters directed the consciences of the Brothers, and especially devoted himself to the spiritual training of the Novices, but he would not take upon him any other authority. So far from directing others, he would do nothing himself without permission; if any one applied to him for advice or direction, he sent him to the Superior, saying, "I am nothing; do not come to me about such things. I will have nothing more to do but to think of death, and weep for my sins." In truth, his whole bearing was that of a penitent sinner, who counted himself unworthy to mix with other men.

But he was called from his retirement at Saint Yon by a matter of business which required his attention and his presence in Paris. A certain M. Rogier, one of those who, though a professing friend and trusted as such, had been instrumental in doing him a great wrong five years before, died, and in his will bequeathed to him, as Superior of the Christian Brothers, a considerable legacy, with an acknowledgment of the wrong he had done, and as some kind of reparation. Legal formalities, somewhat complicated by the fact that he was no longer Superior, and would not claim the legacy under that title, had to be gone through before he could profit by it. He was at first unwilling to take any part in the matter, but at the command of the Superior he went to Paris for the purpose.

He would not go to the Christian Brothers there, fearing that he might not be able to break down their old habit of deference to himself, but he asked for a lodging in the Seminary of Saint Nicolas du Chardonnet, where he counted on being nobody. The holiness, devotion, and humility of his life could not, however, escape notice, and after his death the priests of the Seminary bore witness to the edification his example had been to them all.

In spite of his age and infirmities, he conformed in every particular to the Rule of the house. Rose at the appointed hour, and was first at all religious exercises and devotions. It was winter, but he would not have a room with a fireplace, and at recreation time, instead of joining those who were gathered round the fire to warm themselves, he kept aloof, and would employ the time in talking to one or another of the young Seminarists, trying to help them, and to inspire them with more fervent love to God. In conversation he spoke little, and never of himself or his work ; he was always ready to ask advice of others, and was generally guided by their judgment. He seemed to have completely forgotten what he had been, and what he had done. He looked upon himself as the last and the least ; and although of course the Superiors of the house would have desired that he should do just as he pleased, he never would go out, or speak to any one not belonging to the house without permission. He spent two or three hours a day in meditation, and used to say that he was a very Novice in the way of perfection, and had need to employ the leisure he then enjoyed in learning again the things which he had been taught fifty years before at Saint Sulpice, and which he had forgotten.

The legal business concerning the legacy was tedious, but it was completed at last, and just at a time when the money came in most usefully for the advantage of the Community. Saint Yon, it will be remembered, was only a hired house, belonging to Madame de Louvois, sister-in-law of the Archbishop of Rheims, who had let it on very advantageous terms to M. de la Salle. She had lately died, and the house was to be sold in order to effect the division of her property among her heirs. The place was so admirably adapted to the purposes of the Community that it would have been a very serious inconvenience to leave it, not to speak of the difficulty of finding another suited to their needs. Happily, M. Rogier's legacy enabled them to buy it, and thus at last the Institute became possessed of a permanent home. De la Salle's presence in Paris was of great use in forwarding this transaction.

When all was completed, the Brothers at Saint Yon begged him to return, but he was reluctant to leave Saint Nicolas, where he had been received with so much kindness, and had found rest and peace. He wrote to Frère Barthelemy—

"I am a useless man, and the Institute may thank Heaven that it is rid of me. I need to be guided, and not to guide. It is time that I should begin the work of my own sanctification, after having worked so long at that of others. Since God has given me such a good opportunity, it is for me to make use of it. If I let it slip, it would be a fault for which I should reproach myself for the rest of my days. I have been long enough obliged to command; the time is now come for me to obey, and I would teach you by my example to love a position of dependence better than one of authority. Now that I am happily escaped from all cares that do not concern my salvation, and freed from all those distractions which interrupt communion with God, why should I put myself in the way of them again, and so disturb the sweet repose which I enjoy? All things considered, I am inclined to end my days where I am."

But the Brothers could not bear to think of his ending his days in a strange house, away from them all; and those with whom he was staying, glad as they were to have him, and willingly as they would have kept him, could not deny that his proper place was amongst his own children. At last Frère Barthelemy came to Paris to represent to him how earnestly they desired his return; and yielding at once to his authority, he made no further objection, but accompanied him back to Rouen on the 7th of March, 1718.

It was not to be for long; the good man's infirmities were rapidly increasing upon him. The rheumatism originally caused by the cold and damp of his first poor little house at Vaugirard, and from which he had suffered so severely at Grenoble, as well as at other times, caused him constant pain in all his limbs; he was also subject to asthma. These complaints, it is true, are more commonly the accompaniments of old age than symptoms of approaching death; but the earthly house of his tabernacle was worn out before his time, and he had an inward conviction that death was not far off. He writes to one from whom he had had a letter consulting him about some matter:—

"I entreat you for the love of God, my dear Brother, do not for the future apply to me about anything. You have your Superiors to whom you ought to communicate your affairs, both spiritual and temporal. I desire henceforth to think of nothing but death, which must soon separate me from all creatures."

The same thought transpired in all his conversation; but while dwelling constantly in his own mind on the approach of death, and freely alluding to it in his talk, he was always careful not to betray, by look or manner, the pains which he was suffering; his countenance was ever serene and cheerful, and he relaxed nothing of his accustomed devotions or austerities. Thus he passed the rest of the year 1718 and the first months of 1719.

When Lent began he would have no dispensation from the ordinary rules of fasting and abstinence. "The victim is ready to be offered," he said, "but it must needs be purified." However, his strength declined so rapidly, and his difficulty of breathing became so great, that he was forbidden by his confessor to fast. He obeyed without hesitation. Shortly after, a severe blow on his head caused by the fall of a door, brought on violent pain in the head and side, and his medical attendant did not conceal from him that recovery was not to be expected.

He received this news with joy, but submitted patiently to all the remedies employed, some of them partaking of the barbarous character of those days.

The Festival of St. Joseph, 19th of March, was approaching. He had always had a special veneration for that great Saint, whom he had chosen for Patron of his Society, and he had a great wish to celebrate once more on that Festival. He could hardly have hoped to do so, for he had now for some time been quite unable to leave his bed; but in the evening of the 18th, about ten o'clock, his pain was unexpectedly relieved, and he was conscious of some return of strength. The night was quiet, and on the morning of the Festival he was able to crawl to the Altar, and to celebrate the Holy Mysteries in the presence of all the Brothers, who could hardly believe their eyes. All that day he continued better, was able to converse with the Brothers, listened for the last time to their confidential talk, and gave them some last counsels. But the pain came on again, and he was obliged to go back to bed.

The Curé of the parish, hearing that he was worse, hastened to visit him, and thinking from the bright cheerfulness of his face, that the dying man was not aware of his own condition, said to him, "Do you know that you are dying, and must soon appear before the presence of God?" "I know it," was the answer, "and I wait His commands; my lot is in His hands, His will be done." In truth, his soul dwelt continually in unbroken communion with God, and he only waited with longing for the moment when the last ties that bound him to earth should be severed. Some days passed thus. Feeling that he was getting worse, he asked for the Viaticum, and it was arranged that he should receive it on the following day, which was Wednesday in Holy Week. He spent the whole night in preparation, and his little cell was decorated as well as the poverty of the house allowed. When the time came, he insisted on being taken out of bed, and dressed, and placed in a chair, vested in a surplice and stole. At the sound of the bell announcing the approach of the Priest, he threw himself on his knees, and received his last Communion with the same wonderful devotion which had often formerly struck those who assisted at his Mass, only with even more of the fire of love in his face. It was the last gleam of a dying light, which was being extinguished on earth, to shine with undimmed brightness "as the stars for ever and ever."

The next day, Holy Thursday, he received Extreme Unction. His mind was still quite clear, and the Superior asked him to give his blessing to the Brothers who were kneeling round him, as well as to all the rest of the Community. He raised his eyes to Heaven, stretched out his hands, and said, "The Lord bless you all."

Later in the day he became unconscious, and the prayers for the dying were said, but again he revived. About midnight the death agony came on. It was the night of the Agony in Gethsemane. It lasted till after two; then there was another interval of comparative ease, and he was able to speak. The Superior asked him whether he accepted willingly all his sufferings. "Yes," he replied ; " I adore in all things the dealings of God with me." These were his last words ; at three o'clock the agony returned, but only for a short hour. At four o'clock in the morning of Good Friday, the 7th of April, 1719, he fell asleep.

As soon as the news of his death was spread abroad, the house was beset by crowds desiring to see him. All revered him as a Saint, and wanted to look once more on the venerable face, and to carry away something in remembrance of him. He had nothing belonging to him but a Crucifix, a New Testament, and a copy of the Imitation, but his poor garments were cut up, and distributed in little bits to satisfy the people.

The near approach of the Easter Festival made it desirable that the funeral should take place as soon as possible ; so on the great Sabbath, on which the Master slept after His hard-won victory, the tired servant was laid to rest, very quietly, without any funeral pomp, in a side chapel of the Church of Saint Severus.

The coffin was twice moved—first to the church belonging to the Community of Saint Yon, and afterwards to a chapel of theirs in the town of Rouen, where his body now awaits the resurrection of the just.

CHAPTER XVIII.

THE REVOLUTION.

1720–1833.

AT the time of the founder's death the Institute of the Christian Brothers numbered twenty-seven houses, two hundred and seventy-four Brothers, with nine thousand eight hundred and eighty-five scholars under their care.*

The Frère Barthelemy only survived his beloved master fourteen months. The next Superior was the Frère Timothée, head of the house at Avignon, who was elected on the 15th of August, 1720. With much difficulty, and after many delays, he succeeded in obtaining from the king, Louis XV., letters patent giving legal recognition to the Institute, as an authorized corporation capable of holding property of its own, thereby securing its undisturbed possession of all charitable gifts, legacies, etc.

About the same time, the Pope, Benedict XIII.,

* M. Poujoulat, "Vie du Frère Philippe."

conferred upon it his Apostolic approbation, raising it to the rank of a Religious Order, confirming the Rule in every particular, and thus permanently establishing that peculiar character which the venerable founder had impressed upon it, and had desired that it should always maintain.

Reinforced by this double sanction of Church and State, the work of the Institute grew and developed rapidly. Under the able and vigorous rule of Frère Timothée seventy additional houses were established, and in the year 1789 the number of branch houses had increased to a hundred and twenty-one, there were eight hundred Brothers, and thirty-six thousand children were taught in their schools.

All who in those troubled days were faithful to the Church and to the Faith, not only the Bishops and clergy, but Christian nobles and landed proprietors, encouraged them to the utmost. The Archbishop of Arles, in an address to the Christian Brothers on the occasion of opening a school in his Diocese, spoke thus :—

"You see, dear Brothers, the eagerness with which you are welcomed; every face is radiant with joy. I doubt not that the Lord will bless your labours; you are come to teach the poor, that precious portion of the flock of Jesus Christ, which the Divine Shepherd cherished so tenderly, and which, after His example, you too love from the bottom of your hearts."

Very different language this from that of the

anti-Christian philosophers of the same period, who, under the leadership of Voltaire, were attacking Christianity and the Church on every side; and while talking loudly of liberty, and equality, and the rights of men, despised the poor, scorned the humble and lowly, and said of the labouring folk, " They are like oxen; all they require is a goad, a yoke, and some hay." *

When the fierce storm of the Revolution burst upon France, and, like a tornado, swept over the land, destroying and uprooting all that was best and most sacred in the institutions of the country, it was not possible that the Society of the Christian Brothers should escape its fury. Goaded into madness by frightful wrongs and sufferings, the people were like enraged animals who make no distinction between friends and foes, but rush blindly at all who come in their way. For a time there was respite. The decree of the National Assembly of the 13th of February, 1790, for the suppression of all Religious Orders and congregations of both sexes, made at first an exception in favour of " those engaged in public instruction, and the care of the sick," and there seemed room to hope that those who professed to be taking the side of the people, and reforming the abuses under which they had suffered so long and so terribly, might feel the inconsistency of attacking men whose whole lives

* Letter of Voltaire, of 17th of April, 1766.

were devoted to the service of the humblest classes of the community. But the evil passions at that time let loose cared as little for consistency as for justice, mercy, and truth; and the disciples of Voltaire had learned to look upon the education of the labouring classes as an evil. After a course of constant persecution, false accusations, and the suppression here and there, on one pretence or on another, of several of their houses, a decree was passed by the National Assembly, in the year 1792, abolishing all corporations without exception, whether secular or religious (specifying the Christian Brothers by name), on the ground that "a really free State ought not to allow any kind of corporation, not even those which are devoted to public instruction, and have deserved well of their country." Even while suppressing them, their enemies could not withhold this testimony; but it is hard to understand how the liberty of the State was promoted by preventing the humble Brothers from devoting themselves to the service of the poor and ignorant. " I am a teacher dedicated to the education of the children of the poor. If your protestations of attachment to the people are sincere, and your principles of brotherhood not merely empty words, my office should be my justification, and should deserve your gratitude." Such was the simple defence of a Brother before the Revolutionary tribunal at Avignon. His brave words cost him his life, or, rather, were of no avail to avert the prejudged sentence of death. During the reign of terror and of blood many suffered; more than once it happened that one who was being led out to execution was saved by a member of the National Guard, who had perhaps been taught in one of their schools. The Superior was thrown into prison, the Institute was broken up, the Brothers scattered, and their good work stopped. Many of them still carried on educational work as private teachers on their own account; some found homes as tutors in Christian families. Others were obliged to take to any profession which opened to them a means of livelihood; some entered the army, and of these, two at least attained the rank of generals, and one was raised to the peerage.* Others were equally successful in mercantile affairs. A French emigrant to New York entered the service of a steamship company on the Mississippi; he soon rose to be captain of one of the boats; after a few years he became owner of a boat, shortly after of a second, and before very long twenty vessels belonged to him. He was very hard working, prudent, and intelligent, and his wealth increased rapidly; he bore no name but that of John Peter, he had no one belonging to him, and nobody knew anything about him. Though making money so fast, his life was simple in the extreme,

* "Les Frères des Écoles Chrétiennes," par le General Baron Ambert.

almost to austerity. There was a mystery about him which puzzled the Americans, but he won universal respect and regard for his intelligence and uprightness in business, and his kindness and readiness to help others. At last he died, leaving an enormous fortune. In the hired room where he had lodged for many a year, there was a small wooden trunk; it was opened after his death, and was found to contain his will, and the habit of a Christian Brother. All the millions which he had acquired by his industry and prudence were left to different charities; there was not a single cent which was not bequeathed to the poor; and in his will he desired that he might be buried in the coarse black habit of his Order. Thus under the most untoward circumstances he fulfilled his vow of spending his life in the service of the poor.

The sudden revulsion of feeling in Paris, which on the 9 Thermidor (27th of July, 1794), led to the overthrow of Robespierre, and opened the prison doors to so many victims who were only waiting the moment when they should be led out to the guillotine, brought release to the Superior of the Christian Brothers, after eighteen months' imprisonment. But his Community had ceased to exist; it was to all appearance stamped out. He left Paris and withdrew to Tours, where he remained in complete retirement, till his death in the year 1797. During his imprisonment, Pope Pius VI. had made the Brother who was in charge of the schools at Rome, a sort of Vicar General of the Order, and given him authority to exercise the functions of the Superior till another should be canonically elected, which in the scattered and disorganized state of the Institute it was then impossible to do. He continued in this temporary office till the storm of the Revolution had abated.

Under the government of the First Consul, the Institute began to revive. A law was passed in 1802, giving permission to the Christian Brothers to resume their work of popular education; and although they no longer existed as a corporation in France, and every one of their houses had been suppressed, the scattered members of the Community began to find one another out, and to draw together again; and first at Lyons, afterwards at Paris, and then in various other towns throughout France, two or three were found ready to open schools again, and begin anew the work of Christian education, more than ever needed in the unhappy land over which the blighting storm of irreligion and atheism had so lately passed.

The keen and far-seeing mind of the first Napoleon soon took in the value of such an Institution to the country. Portalis, the Minister of Public Worship, when he became emperor, called his attention to it; and when those who were still opposed to them argued against any recognition or protection being afforded to the Christian Brothers by the Government, Napoleon answered in these words:—

> "I cannot understand the kind of fanaticism with which some people are possessed against the Brothers. It is really prejudice. Petitions come to me from all quarters for their re-establishment. This general demand is a sufficient proof of their utility. The least that can be asked by the Catholics certainly is equality, and thirty millions of men deserve as much consideration as three millions. It is said that the rule which is imposed on the Brothers to abstain from all learning beyond reading, writing, and the elements of arithmetic, is a proof that their influence has always been dreaded. This argument is childish; the only object of this rule is to make them more fit for their vocation."

As the wreck and havoc caused by the Revolution began to be repaired, and society in France was gradually re-organizing itself, it became evident how much need there was of teachers for the people, and the demand for the Christian Brothers far exceeded the supply. It was a case of the harvest being plenteous, but the labourers few. Many members of the dispersed Community were still living, hidden and unknown, here and there about the country; if they could be reassembled something might be done. With this object, the Cardinal Archbishop of Lyons wrote a circular letter addressed to the members of the Institute, appealing to them by their zeal for the glory of God, the salvation of souls, and their own duty, to come to Lyons as soon as possible, in order that they might be employed in the work proper to them.

Many responded to this appeal, and in 1805 twenty houses were re-established in different districts of France. In 1810 Frère Gerband was elected Superior, and the Institute began to recover the full development of its proper organization.

In 1819 they had so won the hearts of the people of Paris, that the municipal council purchased a house in the Faubourg Saint Martin, in order to make it over to the Institute, to be possessed by them free of all rent, as long as the Community should continue there. This house continued to be the mother house of the Institute until the year 1847, when it had to be pulled down to make way for the terminus of the Strasburg Railway, and the house now belonging to them in the Rue Oudinot* was given in exchange.

Difficulties and conflicts still arose from time to time between them and the Government; and in the Revolution of 1830 the Institute received another shock. Though there was not the same violence and persecution as before, the irreligious and anti-Catholic spirits of the time attacked the Christian Brothers through the press, held them up to ridicule, and stirred up against them all the opposition they could. Government grants of money were withdrawn from forty of their houses; eleven

---

* Since this was written the house in the Rue Oudinot has been seized by the Government, and the Brothers driven out.

of these were permanently closed, the rest were supported by private beneficence; everything of the nature of a privilege was withdrawn from them, and they were only tolerated on the same footing as any private lay teachers.

Notwithstanding these discouragements their numbers increased, their schools prospered, and a new branch of work, namely, night schools for adults, was undertaken, and carried on with such marked success that it attracted the attention of M. Guizot, then Minister of Public Instruction, and in February, 1833, he addressed the following letter to the Superior :—

"MONSIEUR,

"Free schools and public lectures, specially intended for adults and artizans, have been opened some time since in different parts of Paris. It is my purpose not only to encourage these praiseworthy efforts for the public instruction of adults among the working classes, but also to stablish and perfect, by the direct intervention of the Government, that which hitherto has not been able to go beyond tentative and somewhat precarious efforts.

"I am aware, Monsieur, with what zeal and intelligence the Christian Brothers have already engaged in this work. I am acquainted with five schools for adults under their management, and in which they assemble every evening more than seven hundred working men. But I have reason to believe that the information I have received on this subject is incomplete; and before I put in operation the means which are in my power to promote the development and efficiency which are to be desired for this class of instruction, it is needful that I should know exactly, on the one hand what has been already done, and on the other what extension could be given to the work by those religious and philanthropic associations which have made so good a beginning.

"I beg of you, therefore, Monsieur, to be so good as to supply me with the information which I desire on those points with which I am concerned, by replying to the following questions :—

"1. How many adult schools have the Brothers opened in Paris?

"2. In what localities, on what days, and at what hours are these schools held?

"3. What are the subjects, and the limits of the instruction given in each school?

"4. What is the number of scholars in each school, and what is the condition or profession to which they belong?

"5. Could the Brothers, with my support, open more adult schools? How many, and in what districts?

"I have no doubt, Monsieur, that with your accustomed zeal you will avail yourself of this opportunity to extend the charitable work to which you have already so noiselessly devoted your labours. I await from you such a prompt and accurate reply as shall put me in a position to act with good effect."

And on receipt of the Superior's answer, he wrote again :—

"Monsieur,

"I have received the letter of the 17th inst., which you have done me the honour to write to me in answer to my inquiries concerning the adult schools conducted by the Brothers of your Institute. I have learned with much satisfaction that your efforts have already had such good results, since seven hundred and ninety working men of all classes are at this moment receiving instruction in your establishments, and that you are on the point of completing arrangements which will allow of your increasing the number.

"I beg of you, Monsieur, to pursue with unabated zeal the

accomplishment of the honourable task which you have taken upon you. I expect further information bearing on all that has as yet been done for the instruction of adults. As soon as I shall have received all the replies which have yet to be made on this most interesting subject, I shall hasten to place at your disposal all the assistance which you may require, and I shall esteem myself happy in thus contributing to the good work which you have set before yourselves."

This promise was fulfilled before long by an annual grant of eight thousand four hundred francs, which, coupled with such words of approbation, all the more valuable as coming from a Protestant Minister, encouraged and enabled the Superior to increase the number and add to the efficiency of the night schools. But it was under the able administration of his great successor, the Frère Philippe, that they attained that successful development which made them so remarkable a feature of the popular educational work of France.

Besides his words of approval, M. Guizot more than once endeavoured to persuade the Superior, Frère Anaclet, to accept the Cross of the Legion of Honour, but it was always declined as being inconsistent with the spirit of the rules of the saintly founder of the Institute.

Thirty-eight years later, after the disasters of the Prussian invasion in 1871, the City of Boston, in America, placed at the disposal of the French Academy a special prize of two thousand francs to be given to whoever should be judged most worthy of the honour, on account of services rendered during the siege and in presence of the enemy. The Academy could find no more fitting recipient of this distinction than the Community, which during the whole time of the war had sent five hundred infirmarians into the battle-fields, one of whom had fallen under the fire of the Prussians, among the wounded at Bourget. This time the Superior was not consulted, and public opinion fully endorsed the decision, when the first literary body in the world adjudged this reward to the humble and despised corps of the Frères des Écoles Chrétiennes. At the same time the National Defence Government insisted on decorating their venerable Superior with a cross of honour. He would have refused it, as he and his predecessor had already done many times, and he only yielded when he was told that there was nothing personal in the honour; that it belonged to his Institute; and that it was only as the representative of the Society that he was asked to wear it. The eminent Dr. Ricord, who had been an eye-witness of the devotion of the Brothers, was charged with the office of fastening the cross on the cassock of Frère Philippe, in the great hall of the mother house. This was the most embarrassing moment in the life of that man of God. He could not bear to wear the cross of honour, and in fact he never did wear it. When he returned after conducting the Doctor to the door at the end of the ceremony, he somehow managed that no one should perceive his decoration. The cross was not to be seen; and it has remained ever since as a kind of myth, or mysterious souvenir; it was never found.

CHAPTER XIX.

FRERE PHILIPPE.

1838–1848.

THE election of the Frère Philippe to the office of Superior on the 21st of November, 1838, forms an epoch in the history of the Christian Brothers. Under his government a new and vigorous life seemed to be infused into the work of the Venerable * De la Salle. He grasped with the intuition of real genius not only the possibilities of extension and development of which the Institute was capable, but also the difficulties and obstacles likely to arise; with the power of a master mind, he averted some hindrances, faced and conquered others, and by the force of a strong will, which in him was ever coupled with a holy humility, those possibilities became accomplished facts.

* The title "Venerable" was conferred on J. B. de la Salle by Pope Gregory XVI. in the year 1840, when application was made to the court of Rome for his Canonization. The question is still before the Congregation of Rites.

We can only glance very briefly at the different branches of new or enlarged work in which the Institute was engaged under his guidance, culminating as they did in that heroic act of Christian charity and exalted patriotism, to which allusion was made in the last chapter, and which, it might have been expected, would alone have been sufficient to give the Christian Brothers a safe place in the hearts of their countrymen, and to shield them from the indignities and ill-usage to which they have, nevertheless, been since exposed.

One of the Frère Philippe's first cares as Superior was to revise and improve the text-books in use in the schools. This he did with so much ability that they were highly commended as the best existing books of the kind by one of the general Inspectors of the University, and they were adopted in many schools unconnected with the Institute. But it was not the books alone which were improved; the living members of the Community felt the elevating, perfecting influence of the example and teaching of their Superior. A current of fresh life and energy seemed to flow from the head and circulate through the whole body, manifesting itself in the increased zeal and higher spiritual life of the several members, as well as in the greater force and efficiency of the Institute as a whole.

This renewed energy found scope in the multiplication and improvement of night schools, commercial schools, industrial schools, boarding schools, and clubs for lads who had left school, where by useful and attractive lectures, innocent entertainments, and religious instruction, the Brothers kept a hold over their former pupils, and guarded them from many of the special dangers and temptations which encompass young men in that particular stage of life. There was also the Institution of Saint Nicolas, a most interesting work, to which a whole volume might well be devoted, but of which only the slightest outline can be given here. The special object of this great work was the rescue and Christian training of the "gamins" of Paris. It was first started in 1827 by a good Priest, M. de Bervanger, who began by gathering seven little street Arabs into the garrets of a house in the Faubourg Saint Marceau; the children were under the charge of a worthy artizan, who taught them and made them work, while his wife did the part of matron. After a few months the little family had outgrown the poor lodging, and means were found to hire a house for them at Vaugirard. In 1833 the numbers had increased tenfold; seventy boys were provided for, and soon after another change became necessary to accommodate a hundred children. So the work grew. One of a noble family, Count Victor de Noailles, having accidentally, as men say, become interested in the case of a poor little boy, for whose safety and education he wished to provide, was advised by the Abbé de Lamennais to apply to M. de Bervanger, and this introduction was the beginning of a life-long friendship. The Count not only contributed largely to the support of the institution, but became himself a zealous and devoted fellow-worker in it. He managed its affairs, collected contributions, and himself supplied all deficiencies in the funds, while M. de Bervanger superintended both the children and the masters, was with them in the refectory and in the playground, gave the religious instruction, and watched over all the details of the inner life of the house. Under the joint protection of the two friends, the establishment prospered so much that in a few years there were eleven hundred boys, who all received a good primary education, with careful religious training and instruction, and when old enough were apprenticed to different trades, and not sent out into the world till they were in a position to earn good wages as carpenters, joiners, turners, watchmakers, etc.

Count Victor de Noailles died in 1837, and for twenty years M. de Bervanger carried on the management alone, but he found the burden of so large a concern too heavy for his advancing years. It was a hard struggle to resign the direction of a work of which he had been the originator, which had been so blessed under his care, and in which his whole heart had been for so many years wrapped up, loving and caring for every one of that large family as if they were his own children. But that very love, truly parental in its self-sacrifice, enabled him to overcome all selfish reluctance, and though not without effort, he placed his resignation in the hands of the Archbishop of Paris.

The Archbishop saw at once that nothing would so tend to secure the permanence and perfection of the work as to put it under the charge of the Christian Brothers, if they could be induced to undertake it. After careful inquiry, the Superior consented to do so, and on the 10th of April, 1859, the Brothers were formally installed by the Cardinal Archbishop of Paris, and the governing council of the institution. The importance of this undertaking may be gathered from the fact that the staff of Brothers required at first starting was seventy. Twenty years later there were a hundred and thirty engaged in the Institution, which consisted of three separate houses: one at Issy, a village about twelve miles from Paris, on the road to Versailles, where the little boys were received at the age of seven years, and kept at school and under religious instruction till after their first Communion—this house contained nine hundred children; there was another house at Igny, in the Department of Seine and Oise, where two hundred boys were employed in gardening and agriculture; and a third in Paris, in the Rue Vaugirard, where nearly a thousand were taught various trades.

It will be in the memory of many that one of the saddest incidents of the siege of Paris in 1871, was the bursting of a shell in one of the dormitories of this house, whereby five children were killed and others terribly mutilated. When the bombardment began on that side of the city, the Frère Directeur of Saint Nicolas wrote to all the parents, requesting them to remove their children if they thought it safer to do so. About two hundred were withdrawn, but far the greater number were left in the Brothers' charge. The scarcity caused by the siege was at this time pressing heavily; food had reached famine prices,[*] many were dying of want, and to the parents of these children it was a serious matter to have one additional mouth to feed. At Saint Nicolas, thanks to the foresight and good management of the Brothers, the provisions never failed.

All necessary precautions were taken to guard against the dangers of the bombardment, mattresses were placed in the windows, and tubs of water throughout the house in case of fire.

On the night of the 9th of January, or rather in the early morning of the 10th, the discharge of bombs and shells in the neighbourhood of the house was so incessant that it was decided to move all

---

[*] On the 1st of January, 1871, a chicken cost 60 francs; a rabbit, 35 frs.; a goose, 140 frs.; a cat, 20 frs.; a rat, 2 frs.; an egg, 2 frs.; a turnip, 2 frs.; a pound of butter, 40 frs.

the children into the cellars for safety. It was about one o'clock in the morning, and hundreds of children had to be roused and dressed. Before this could be accomplished, the fatal tragedy occurred; in another quarter of an hour all would have been saved.

A touching account is given of one of the little sufferers, whose thigh was so frightfully injured that it was necessary to take it off from the hip-joint. The poor child, who was conscious throughout, asked to see one of the Brothers who had been his teacher; and when he came into the room, stretched out his little hand, thanking him affectionately for all his kindness, and saying, "Dear Brother, let us shake hands once more." Just then the Blessed Sacrament was brought to him by one of the Curates of the parish. Before communicating he wished to make his confession; the Priest desired him not to attempt more than to lift up his heart with him to God to ask pardon for his faults. "Oh," replied the little sufferer, "I can very well make my act of contrition myself." A few hours afterwards he expired, having devoutly and with full consciousness received the last Sacraments." *

By the kindness of the Frère Directeur, the writer was allowed to visit this great Institution in the month of June of the present year, and was most

* "Les Frères des Écoles Chrétiènnes," pendant la guerre par J. D'Arsac.

kindly and courteously conducted over every part of the building by one of the Brothers. It consists of a large quadrangle, enclosing a spacious court, which serves as a playground, and is well shaded by thickly growing plane trees. On the first floor, each side of the quadrangle is traversed by a gallery or passage, on either side of which are class-rooms adapted to hold from forty to forty-five boys, and each presided over by a Brother. Here the different lessons were going on. Above are the dormitories, with lavatories attached. In one of the dormitories is still plainly to be seen the mark in the ceiling of the place where the shell came in.

On this floor are also the workshops, where the boys who are old enough, and have gone through their school course, learn various trades. Carpenters, shoemakers, carvers, gilders, bookbinders, musical instrument makers, opticians, and others were all busily at work. The Brothers, of course, have nothing to do with this department of the boys' education, but it is managed so as to be no expense to the Institution. Skilled artizans from the town are glad to undertake it, on condition that they have whatever profit they can make of the boys' work.

At the time of the writer's visit, there were nine hundred and fifty boys in the house, about fifty *employés* for the service of the kitchen and other household work, and a hundred Brothers in charge. Six hundred names were inscribed, waiting for admission, and two thousand applications had been refused for want of room. Boys are received at the age of seven years; the payment made for them varies according to circumstances from thirty to forty francs a month. It may be said to average a shilling a day. For this moderate sum they are lodged, clothed, fed, and cared for in every way. Their education, of course, costs nothing, as it is given by those who take no pay.

A more joyous, merry, noisy troop it would be hard to see than that which poured into the playground at four o'clock (the hour for closing school) in the afternoon of Friday, 29th of June, 1883. But the tongues, which gave signs of a full share of the national volubility, are under strict control; a rule of silence is enforced on the stairs and in the dormitories from the time when they are dismissed for the night till the morning's work begins again, and it is strictly observed.

A very interesting educational experiment was made under the government of the Frère Philippe, by the admission of blind, and deaf and dumb children into the ordinary schools. Much had already been done for these afflicted ones, but only apart, by themselves; it was not thought possible to teach them with other children. It was a bold experiment, but when tried it had the happiest results. Contact with others both at lessons and at play seemed to lift a cloud from their minds, and to dispel the timid reserve, and sense of isolation which crushed down the spring of their young life. A very few weeks' study and training were found sufficient to enable the masters to deal with them. They were received at the same age as the others, and kept till their first Communion, after which they were received into the institutions specially designed for them, and were found to have a capacity and intelligence far beyond those who had not mixed with others.

Another most important work entrusted to the Christian Brothers during the Superiorship of the Frère Philippe, was the charge of prisoners. The first attempt of this kind was made at Nîmes, in the year 1841. At the request of the local authorities, the Minister of the Interior applied to the Superior, and he consented to make trial of the plan, but not without mature deliberation, and laying down certain conditions, by which he hoped to secure freedom of action for the Brothers. At first only the young prisoners, lads of from sixteen to eighteen years of age, were committed to their charge, and before long the whole condition of things was changed in their quarter of the house. But besides these, there were twelve hundred adult convicts under the charge of warders, who treated them with the harsh brutality too common in men of their class. At chapel the contrast was most striking between these poor men, guarded by twenty armed jailors, and the band of youthful offenders, under no superintendence but that of two religious Brothers, who unarmed, but with books of devotion in their hands, knelt at the head of their little flock.

The wonderful improvement visible in these poor lads naturally inspired the wish that the care of all the prisoners might be put into the hands of the Christian Brothers. It was plain that the convicts themselves wished it, and persons of weight and influence at Nimes asked for it. The Superior had grave doubts how far it would do to place his Brothers in a position of such tremendous difficulty; he feared lest they might not be equal to the management of twelve hundred criminals. How could the superintendence of such a multitude be effectively carried on, in the refectory, or in the dormitories? In case of a revolt amongst them, what could be done, even with the help of nine sentries and fifty soldiers stationed in the establishment? There would be danger in the nightly rounds of inspection, and great difficulty in enforcing punishment for misdemeanours. Added to all this there was the danger of conflict between the authority of the Brothers and that of the lay officials, and also there was the question how, under such a charge, the religious Brothers were to find time for the spiritual exercises and devotions to which they were bound by their rule.

No wonder the Superior hesitated; it is rather a wonder to learn that, after having well considered the subject in all its bearings, and taken such precautions as lay in his power, to the great joy of the authorities, he gave an affirmative answer to their request; and early in the year 1842 the rough prison warders gave place to the gentle Brothers. In the course of two months the whole character of the prison, or house of correction, was altered, and a troop of convicts might be seen following a Brother to their prison cells as meekly as sheep follow their shepherd. Instead of being guarded by men of fierce and threatening aspect, who were never without their swords, and ruled them by fear alone, addressing them in words of contempt, intermingled with oaths and imprecations, the convicts found themselves watched over by unarmed men, who with no means whatever of defence, yet moved fearlessly among them, always gentle and quiet in manner, speaking to them, with a sweet smile, words of kindness, calling them "brothers," and encouraging them to resignation and hope. They found *themselves* actually addressing as "*dear brothers*" the men whose duty it was never to lose sight of them. This word "brothers" had a wonderful power. They had thought they were outcasts from society, and they found they had brothers! They were lifted in their own sight out of the degradation in which they were sunk; they felt capable of becoming better. The sight of these men who came and buried themselves in the prison with the one purpose of being of use to them, and who for no human interest, but simply for the love of God, gave themselves up of their own free will to such a hard and revolting task, first astounded them, then made them think, and kindled a feeling of gratitude in their hearts. They tried to do well in order to please the Brothers. They heard of God, of His mercy, of a life to come, of restoration through repentance, of the hopes, even in this world, attendant on a new life of well-doing. A whole world of thoughts and hopes, long unknown, or at least long forgotten, was opened to them, and the power of the religion of Christ triumphed over those hardened natures.

There was manifest improvement of other kinds also, thus acknowledged by M. Duchatel, Minister of the Interior, in a letter to Frère Philippe:—

"I can never forget that when the Brothers were sent to the central house at Nîmes, that establishment was, in sanitary respects, in a most deplorable condition; and I am convinced that the remarkable improvement in the health of the criminals during the last year must be attributed in great measure to the careful and just superintendence of the Brothers, and to the moral influence which they exert over the prisoners, through the example of their own devotion and through their wise counsels and pious exhortations."

But it did not all work smoothly; difficulties did arise between the secular authorities of the prison and the Brothers, and the friction thus caused checked and retarded the progress of moral and religious improvement. The experience of the first year, though in many points most satisfactory, could not be considered a full success; but there was on both sides an honest wish to conciliate, and some fresh regulations were agreed upon, after friendly consultation between the Superior and the Minister of the Interior, by which the position of the Brothers in the prison was improved, and greater facilities given for their special work of instruction, both secular and religious, and for the moral and spiritual reform, which was their principal aim.

In 1844, another central house of correction was put into their hands, at Fontevrault, where twelve hundred adult criminals and two hundred boys were confined. Forty-eight Brothers were sent there. Two years later, fifty were put in charge of the prison at Melun, and twenty were sent to a smaller house of correction at Aniane.

It must not be supposed that all this could be done without failures, trials, and disappointments. The Brothers had occasionally much to suffer, and one of them was murdered by a convict in the prison at Nîmes; but they had counted the cost before entering on the work, and they were sustained in it by the love of God and of their fellow-men.

After the Revolution of 1848 changes took place in the regulations of the prisons, which made it impossible for the Brothers to carry on their work of love, and the Superior applied to the Home Office for leave to withdraw them. This was granted in September, 1848, with expressions of gratitude for "the devotion which the Brothers had shown, and the services which they had rendered in the prisons."

Thus was cut short an experiment which had, on the whole, been a great success, and which may yet serve, at some future time, as a guide and help towards the solution of the difficult problem, how to make houses of correction real reformatories, instead of hotbeds of vice and misery.

It is impossible within the limits of this volume to enter with any detail into the work of the Christian Brothers in lands beyond their own. We can only note in the briefest manner the marvellous extension of the Institute, under the able administration of Frère Philippe, in every part of the known world; not only in Belgium, Austria, Prussia, Italy, Great Britain, Ireland, and all the countries of Europe, but in the other continents also: in the Levant, India, Cochin China; in Algeria, Madagascar, the Mauritius, Alexandria, Cairo, and the banks of the Nile; and with remarkable success in America, in Canada, the United States, the West Indies, and South America, and in Australia.

The history of each one of these foundations, which succeeded one another with wonderful rapidity in the space of a few years, would furnish matter of deepest interest, and sufficient to fill a volume rather than a chapter; but we must pass on to the crowning act of Frère Philippe's life, by which the devoted charity, the courage and the patriotism of the Brothers, were exhibited to the world under very different circumstances from those of their ordinary life, and in more striking colours than ever before.

CHAPTER XX.

THE WAR AND THE COMMUNE.

1870, 1871.

No sooner had war been declared between France and Prussia, in July, 1870, than the venerable Superior of the Christian Brothers, as if foreseeing the utter lack of preparations of every kind in the French army, wrote to the Minister of War, offering to place all the resources of the Institute at the service of their country; their houses to be used as hospitals for the wounded, the Brothers themselves to act as Infirmarians, either in them or in the Ambulance Service on the battle-fields. "The soldiers love our Brothers," he wrote, "and our Brothers love them; many of them have been brought up in our schools, and will gladly find themselves cared for by their old schoolmasters."

The offer was thankfully accepted. In a very short time all the establishments of the Christian Brothers were ready for the reception of the sick and wounded, and soon all the help they could give was called for, by the disasters of that fatal campaign. Their first call was to supply food, clothing, lint, bandages, everything in short, to the wounded in the bloody engagements round Metz, on the 14th, 16th, and 18th of August. These poor men were gathered hastily from the field of battle, and packed into trains, eight of which, each containing five hundred, arrived at the Thionville Station, utterly unprovided with all necessaries. Of course the resources of the Brothers could not have sufficed for so great a need; but they organized the service for the distribution of the supplies which were liberally contributed by the inhabitants of the town.

Very soon they were called to closer contact with the horrors of war, being employed as ambulance bearers, to carry the wounded from the field, and to wait upon them afterwards. Five hundred Brothers from Paris alone were thus employed. They might be seen early in the morning, setting out with their venerable Superior at their head, who, notwithstanding his fourscore years, never failed to lead them out, and send them forth, encouraged by his words, and strengthened by his blessing, to the work to which he could not follow them.

As to the Brothers, it is said that they stood fire as if they had been used to it all their lives. Their discipline and their courage were acknowledged by all to be equally admirable.

When they reached the scene of the combat, they girded up their loins with a cord, and advanced steadily by two and two, each pair carrying a litter or stretcher. Wherever the fire was hottest they might be seen, making their way to the wounded, carefully lifting them from the ground, and carrying them with all possible precaution to the surgeons and ambulance waggons. Their calm courage struck even old soldiers with admiration. "My Brothers," cried a general on one occasion, "neither humanity nor charity require you to go so far." And an eminent physician was so moved at the sight of their devotion, that he asked, as he clasped the hand of one of the Brothers, "Is kissing allowed amongst you?" "Well, there is no rule exactly about it," replied the Brother. "Allow me, then, to have the honour of embracing you: you are wonderful, you and yours. Take this kiss to Frère Philippe, and all your Brothers, and tell them that we all thank you, in our own name, and in the name of France."

It was on this service that Frère Néthelme, one of the masters of Saint Nicolas, met his death. He and another Brother were carrying a litter for the wounded in the battle of Bourget, when there was a discharge of musketry, the balls whistled round them, and he fell mortally wounded. He was laid on the stretcher which he had been carrying, another took his place, and bore him back to the ambulance. Another Brother was wounded; as he staggered, one who was near sprang forward to support him. "It is nothing," he said; "help those who are in greater need." And when they asked his name, "Why do you ask?" he replied. "I am here to fulfil a duty, for which I look to God alone to reward me, not to the praises of my fellow-creatures."

When the supply of litters or stretchers failed, the Brothers lifted the wounded in their arms, and carried them thus, or on their shoulders long distances. The brave General Renault was one of those whom they carried from the field of Champigny, after his leg had been shattered by the bursting of a shell. "I have grown grey on battlefields," he said to one of the Brothers, "I have been in twenty-two campaigns, but I have never seen so bloody an engagement as this." It was on the same field of bloodshed that a young lieutenant fell, wounded by a ball in the breast. The Brothers went to him immediately. "Ah," he cried when he saw them, "here are the good Brothers; they brought me up, and now they are come to help me on the field of battle." The Brothers spoke some comforting words to him while they gave a hasty dressing to his wound; then they lifted him on their shoulders to carry him to the surgeons. When they had gone a few hundred paces, they told him that a Priest was in sight, coming towards them. "Call him," he said, "I want to make my confession." They hastened on, and soon the Priest was with them. Walking alongside, without stopping their sorrowful march, he heard the young soldier's confession, and gave him absolution; and thus bathed in the precious Blood, he left him happy and full of hope, though his own life blood was flowing fast, and very soon he departed to that land "where nation shall not rise against nation, neither shall they learn war any more."

Sadder and more heart-rending, if possible, was the work of the Brothers when a battle was over, and they had to explore the scene of carnage, to bury the dead, and seek any wounded who might yet survive. They might be seen kneeling on the wet ground, on ice, it might be, or snow, or mud, raising the pale heads, watching for the faintest sign of life from the blanched lips, or for a glance of consciousness in the dying eyes, bringing to those in whom there was still a spark of life, such relief as was possible.

The following graphic account, from the pen of one who had been on the field of Champigny all day,* will give some idea of what this work was. After describing some of the events of the battle, and how when night closed over the scene of

* The Frère Directeur of Montrouge.

carnage, the weary Brothers sought to snatch a short time of rest, some returning home, and others throwing themselves on the straw beside the soldiers, he goes on :—

"As for me, being stronger and more robust than the rest, I got into a waggon and came back to explore the ground of Champigny, Petit Bric, and Tremblay. When I reached the plateau of Noisy, where numbers of wounded were uttering cries of pain and despair, a soldier who was cutting a slice of flesh from the carcase of a horse which had been killed that morning, told me that the Prussians had not allowed the wounded to be removed, and that if I went any farther I should be taken prisoner. My anxiety to bring help to those brave men made me go on in spite of his warning ; but after a few minutes, the fire of a patrol stopped my way, and proved to me that what the soldier said was true. It was one o'clock in the morning. I turned and came back with a heavy heart, as I thought of those unhappy ones lying there, in bitter cold, upon the ground, which was soaked with their blood, and under the searching eye of a cruel enemy. 'Poor young fellows !' I said to myself; 'before the dawn their eyes will perhaps have closed for ever to the light of day ! and they will have died without help or consolation, without even hearing one friendly word.' . . .

"The man who drove my carriage was afraid, and his tired horses would not go on. I left them ; and with a lantern in my hand, I searched the roads, the woods, the open country, but I found only dead bodies. I shouted, and listened ; the silence of death reigned around. At last, guided by the light of the fires, I made my way to the place where our soldiers were bivouacking, and I learned from them that several wounded had been carried towards the close of the day into a house which was still standing, on a height a little above the spot where they were.

"There indeed they lay ; men who had been found in the

trenches or behind the slopes, or who had dragged themselves to the foot of the wall to die; there they were, waiting calmly and patiently till some help should come.... There were twenty-one of these poor sufferers. Happily Providence had not sent me alone to their aid; two other carriages had arrived before mine. We placed them in them as gently and comfortably as we could, and we set out. On the heights of Joinville a Prussian shell burst close to us, and put out our lamps, but did no other mischief. At 4.30 a.m. we had reached Paris, and were in the Rue Saint Antoine, trying to find a lodging for our twenty-one wounded, for the hospitals had all been filled the day before. We found a shelter for them at last, and I set out at once to return to Champigny.

"But what had become of the unfortunate wounded whose cries had pierced my heart, when I could do nothing for them? I went to the plateau of Noisy, and there more than four score frozen corpses told the story of the cruelty of our enemies."

When a suspension of arms was granted for the burial of the dead, it was the Christian Brothers who performed that sad and sacred task. Sixty of them were thus employed after the battle of Champigny. With exhausting toil they dug deep pits from thirty to fifty metres long in the frozen, snow-covered ground, and in these they reverently laid the bodies of the slain, in their uniforms, just as they had fallen. Six hundred and eighty-five soldiers and officers were thus buried. It was night, and the work had to be done by the flickering light of torches. Soon after midnight the Prussian officers who were superintending the interment of their own dead, gave notice that the armistice was about to end. Lime was thrown into the pits, they were hastily filled in, and the falling snow spread its pure winding-sheet over them.

When all was finished, the Brothers brought a large black wooden cross, and planted it upon the grave; they then knelt down, and said the "De profundis." Even the Prussian officers were moved. "We have seen nothing like it before," said one of them. "Except the Grey Sisters," replied another, in a voice which expressed the deepest respect and admiration.

The horrors of disease accompanied those of war; small-pox and fever raged fearfully in some places, and the nursing of the sick called for as great devotion as the care of the wounded, the dying, and the dead. Cases of virulent small-pox, which were given up by the medical men as being past all possibility of recovery, were saved by the devoted and unremitting attention of the Brothers. "I would not do that for a hundred francs an hour," was the exclamation of a soldier, as he watched the tender, unflinching handling of a patient in the most repulsive form of that loathsome disease. "No more would I," replied the Brother infirmarian, "nor for a million; but I would do it with pleasure for the love of God." The poor invalid, who had been pronounced by the doctors to be already in such a state of decomposition that in twelve hours he must be dead, recovered, and lived to thank the

Brother to whose unselfish devotion he owed his life.

It was not in and around Paris alone that the disciples of the Venerable De la Salle exhibited such wonderful courage, devotion, and charity; all over France it was the same. From the beginning of the war to the end, throughout all the Provinces, wherever there was bloodshed or pestilence, they were found, ministering to the suffering; and one remarkable fact must not be omitted, namely, that this service was rendered by them without any neglect of their own proper work. They did not desert their schools, that they might wait upon the sick and wounded; the schools went on regularly; all through the siege of Paris they were never closed. The Brothers seemed to multiply themselves; they sufficed for all—for the school, the hospital, and the battle-field. Each took his turn; one day in the school, the next under fire.

To the horrors of the siege succeeded the far worse horrors of the Commune. The Superior of the Christian Brothers seems to have foreseen what was coming, for he had taken the precaution of dispersing all the Novices before the 18th of March, 1871. He had a presentiment that Paris was going to fall into the hands of worse enemies than the Prussians—enemies of all civilization and all religion. The truly satanic spirit which actuated them was plainly revealed by the words of one of their leaders,

Raoul Rigault: "As long as there shall be a single individual who pronounces the name of God, all will yet remain to be done; there will always be shots to be fired." This was their fearful programme, and during the two months that their power lasted, they did their utmost to carry it out. Their profession of care for the interests of the people ought to have produced some feeling of respect towards the Brothers, whose whole life was consecrated to the good of the working classes; and the services they had rendered on the battle-fields and in the hospitals, might have been expected to win for them protection at least, if not gratitude. But they were Christians; and this in the eyes of the Communists was an unpardonable offence. The Brothers were willing and ready to have nursed the victims of this horrible insurrection, as they had done the soldiers, but they were not allowed to do so; the Communists preferred that their wounded should be left without assistance, rather than they should be attended by them. Members of religious orders and all the clergy were hateful in their eyes, as foul things of which it was their business to rid the world. Two laws were made to facilitate the accomplishment of this business. By the first, all the property of religious bodies was confiscated to the State; and by the other, every able-bodied citizen from nineteen to forty years of age was obliged to serve in the army.

After the arrest of the Archbishop and several of the clergy, information reached the Brothers, that their Superior was on the list of the proscribed, and would shortly be arrested. Upon this, they entreated him to escape while he could, and at the earnest request of his assistants and the heads of the Community, he left Paris to visit some of their houses in the country. The next day a commissary from the Commune with forty of the National Guard entered the mother house, carried away all the money they could find, and some of the altar plate; and finding that the Superior had escaped, they seized the next in authority, the Frère Calixte, and took him to the Préfecture; but before long he was set at liberty. By the goodwill and helpful contrivance of several of the well-disposed inhabitants of Paris, a great many of the Brothers who were of the age for military service escaped. After a time the Communists became suspicious, and watched them more closely, and from thirty to forty of them were arrested at the stations, or at the gates of the town as they were trying to make their escape. Some were released, but twenty-six were imprisoned as hostages.

Their schools, which had gone on all through the siege, were forcibly closed, all accept Saint Nicolas which, wonderful to relate, went on as usual, and through the worst of the time, had three hundred scholars, and thirty Brothers in charge. The mother house of the Institute was taken possession of as a hospital, and fitted up with four hundred beds, and at first the Brothers hoped to be allowed to act as infirmarians to the wounded in their own house. But just as they were about to begin, an order was issued by the committee of public safety, to the effect that not one of the Brothers was to remain in the house, under pain of arrest and imprisonment.

" It was then," wrote Frère Philippe, "that our dear assistant Brothers, and the others who had remained till that moment at the post of danger, as well as our sick and aged, found themselves obliged to leave our house, which could, alas! no longer be called a mother house, but rather a widowed house, and during five or six days, a house of woe and death."

After a week of bloodshed and deadly strife, the insurgents began to give way, and the Brothers were able again to get possession of their mother house and other establishments. Those who had left Paris began to return, but the imprisoned ones were still in the dungeons of Mazas. The saintly Archbishop and the revered Curé of the Madeleine, with others of the clergy, had been murdered, and it was the intention of the insurgents to shoot all their prisoners, and thus to renew in 1871 the massacres of 1792.

But this second reign of terror was drawing to an end. On Thursday, the 25th of May, the army of deliverance broke through the barricades, and as the firing thickened round Mazas the gaolers opened the prison doors, and set free from four to five hundred prisoners. Amongst them were the Brothers who had been seized. But fresh perils awaited them. They found themselves entangled in the lines of the insurgents, and were forced to work at the barricades till they could find opportunity to escape, either under cover of the shades of night, or in some other way eluding the vigilance of their enemies. While thus engaged, one of them was wounded by the bursting of a shell, and died on the spot. The rest escaped; some reached the mother house on Friday, others on Saturday, and two not till Sunday afternoon; they had been forcibly detained by the insurgents. When the victorious army surrounded and disarmed the rebels, they were fettered and chained together in sets of five, and taken before a council of war, sitting at La Roquette. The two poor Brothers had been chained to three insurgents; they had been present at the examination of those who preceded them, and had witnessed the execution of a great number. After three hours of anxious expectation, their turn came. When examined, they told their story: that they were Christian Brothers, who had been let out of prison three days before, but that it had been impossible for them to escape from the insurgents. The council, being satisfied of the truth of their statement, gave them a free pass, and they returned to the mother house, exhausted with fatigue, and with the terrible emotions caused by all they had gone through.

As soon as the insurrection had been put down, an order was issued by the Government for the reopening of all places of public instruction. The conclusion must be given in the Superior's own words:—

"As soon as our Brothers who had fled from Paris were made aware of this order, they made haste to return; they forgot all they had suffered, and only thought of the good which they might now do; and at the moment in which I write, we are again in possession of our Communities and our schools, and at liberty to accomplish the work which is the end and object of our vocation, and which, now more than ever, is of the highest importance for the regeneration of society.

"I returned to Paris on the 9th of June. I cannot express the shock which I experienced when I saw this unhappy city, whose most beautiful monuments and such a great number of houses are nothing but a heap of ruins. Neither can I describe what I felt when I crossed the threshold of our mother house, and found there only Brothers, who threw themselves into my arms, and with me shed tears of mingled sorrow and joy.

"As it was the hour for the Benediction Service, we went and fell down at the feet of our Divine Saviour, laying ourselves low under His gracious hand, and thanking Him with all the overflowing fulness of our hearts for the Providential protection which He had granted to us. After Benediction, the Psalm, 'Ecce quam bonum,' was chanted. How affecting it was to hear under such circumstances the beautiful words of the Psalmist, 'Behold, how good and joyful a thing it is, brethren, to dwell together in unity.'"

CHAPTER XXI.

CONCLUSION.

1871–1883.

BEFORE many days had passed, the schools of the Christian Brothers were opened again, and their various works were in operation, as before the war. The Superior, who looked upon all their sufferings and trials as calls from God to fresh energy and deeper devotion, infused his own holy zeal into the members of the Institute; and before his death, which took place in January, 1874, he had the joy of seeing the ranks of his beloved Community recruited by the admission of fifty-four postulants, who received the habit on the 7th of December, 1873.

The next five years were a time of peace. The Brothers were allowed to carry on their good works without molestation, and in 1878 their numbers had increased to 11,640; they had 1249 establishments, and the number of their scholars was 390,607.*

The character of the education given in their schools may be estimated from the following facts. For the last forty years a certain number of exhibitions or scholarships (bourses) have been offered by the city of Paris for competition amongst the scholars of elementary or primary schools, which give to the successful candidates a right of free education in the higher class schools (école primaire supérieure) in the Chaptal College, or in the School of Arts and Trades. The number of scholarships which are offered varies. In 1848 there were twenty-nine; in 1871, fifty; in 1874, eighty; and in 1877 the number was raised to one hundred. Competition is open † to the pupils of all elementary schools, whether taught by the Christian Brothers or by lay teachers of no religious order or society.

The result, taking the thirty years from 1847 to 1877, has been that of 1445 exhibitions gained by scholars, 1148 have been won by boys from the Christian schools, and 297 by those from other schools. Or to take the last seven years of that period, during which every effort has been made by the Government, at a lavish outlay, to promote the efficiency of the secular schools, the results,

* Le General Baron Ambert, "Les Frères," etc.
† It *was* when these words were written; it is no longer.

though the numbers are not quite so disproportioned, yet show a marked superiority in the schools of the Christian Brothers. Out of 490 exhibitions, 364 have been adjudged to their pupils, and 126 to those of the secular schools.

The subjects of examination are—

1. Moral and religious instruction.
2. Spelling, and writing from dictation.
3. Arithmetic and geometry.
4. History of France.
5. Geography, general, and special of France.
6. Geometrical drawing.
7. Freehand drawing.
8. Writing.
9. Singing.

Nothing is known of the examination papers and questions till the day of trial, and no names of competitors are given; they are only distinguished by numbers. The judges are a committee nominated by the Prefect of the Seine; their disposition would be all on the side of favouring the secular schools as much as possible. Any doubt which might be entertained on this point has been effectually set at rest by the fact that within the last few months the scholars from the Christian schools have been forbidden any more to compete with the others. Their successes made the superiority of the teaching too manifest; it must be kept out of sight.

Character of their Teaching. 269

The enemies of religious instruction have objected that these examinations are not a fair test of the education given in the Brothers' schools, because the competition for prizes is limited to a few select pupils from the advanced classes of the school, and the other children are neglected in order to work up these head boys.

This accusation can best be answered in the words of M. Gréard, Inspector of the University, and director of primary education. He says—

> "If the competition for exhibitions is the test of the select, the examination for certificates is the test of the average. In this case the teacher has to bring the largest possible number of scholars up to the level of that amount of general knowledge which should be the acquisition of every child who has attended school regularly. There is no special preparation; it is by a natural process of gradual advance, without any particular effort beyond the regular application of each day, that the children attain to the certificate, which is the crowning point of their school work. It is, therefore, only by steady daily teaching that masters can secure this success."

Judged by this test, the schools of the Christian Brothers are found to take a much higher place than the Government schools. The average number of certificates obtained by their pupils, from the year 1869 to 1878, has been every year little short of double the number obtained by the pupils of the Government schools.

And surely it is not surprising that it should be so; rather it is what we should expect, that men who are wholly devoted to their work, and whose Community life relieves them of all distractions, should themselves attain to a higher perfection in their art than those who have the cares of family life upon them, and whose minds are disturbed by all those petty daily anxieties which must needs beset the father of a family, and which often cause more distraction than greater and more important matters.

Rising, as their rule requires, at half-past four, they have heard Mass, performed their private devotions, breakfasted, and had an hour or more for study before they begin school. As they never live alone, the housekeeping and cooking are allotted to one or more, according to the size of the establishment; those whose office it is, see to the provisions and keep the accounts. The others have no concern with these matters; they have, therefore, nothing to disturb their studies and devotions, and when the hour for recreation comes, they are free to enjoy it, undistracted by home worries or by home joys.

And besides this, there is the strength and efficiency derived from corporate and united action. All individual personality is abandoned when one joins the Institute. He even parts with his name, and with it of course all desire for renown, all selfish interest even in the success of his work, is given up. Each one is but a unit in a well organized army. At the command of his Superior he goes to a place; by the same authority he is recalled; wherever he is he does the work assigned to him "with his might." The vow of obedience ensures perfect subordination, while at the same time the spirit of a true fraternity and equality is maintained amongst them. The young Novice, who has charge of the cooking and household work for his two companions in a distant department at the foot of the Alps or the Pyrenees, and the Superior who, at his desk in Paris, holds all the threads of the vast Community, and commands an organized army over the whole of France and beyond it, both wear a mantle of the same coarse woollen cloth, and a hat of the same felt, and address one another as " My Brother."

When to these natural causes we add the supernatural, we shall no longer be inclined to wonder at their success. A true Christain Brother, one who has really attained, at least in some degree, to the type set before him by the venerable founder of the Institute, does all his work in a supernatural spirit—that is to say, in a spirit of love. By the grace of a spiritual paternity he has a father's tenderness for the children committed to his charge, and he wins their love simply by loving them. He devotes himself entirely to them, he takes part in their work, in their play, and in their prayers; and love begets love in all, but especially in the fresh young heart of childhood. The heart of a child who is sure of being loved, is quite sure to love again; and who does not know how much more readily children receive and appropriate instruction from one whom they love, than from one whom they only fear? And, to quote the words of another,*—

"If you ask (the Christian Brother) whence he has derived this feeling, at once so grave and so sweet (towards the little ones who must perpetually try his patience), he will tell you, that he has heard in the secret depths of his heart the voice of his own Master, saying, 'These children are dear to Me; be a father, and more than a father, to them. Watch over them tenderly, be just and kind. If thy heart is not large enough to embrace them, I will enlarge it after the pattern of My own: if these young creatures are docile and obedient, bless Me for it: if they are froward, call upon Me for help: if they weary thee, I will be thy Consolation: if thou sink under the burden, I will be thy Reward."

The slight sketch which has been here attempted of the life and character of the venerable founder of the Institute of Frères des Écoles Chrétiennes, and of the subsequent history of his Society, will, it is hoped, be some kind of answer to the question who, and what manner of men they are, out of whose hands the anti-clerical party in France have done what they could to take the education of the young.

They have done what they could—that is to say,

* M. Chesnelong, "L'Education Chrétienne et l'École sans Dieu." Discours prononcé le 15 April, 1879.

Successful efforts of the Church party.

they have driven them from their schools; they have withdrawn from them all public support; they have laid upon the taxpayers of the country an enormous additional burden to pay the new schoolmasters, who instead of the 800 or 1000 francs which sufficed for the Brothers, require 1500 or 2000, not to speak of other sums lavishly expended in the attempt to make the Government schools as effective as the Christian schools, and more attractive to the people.*

But they have not succeeded in their attempt; they have not persuaded the Catholic fathers and mothers of France that a Godless education is better for their children than a religious one. They have not been able to take the education of the children of the people out of the hands of the Christian Brothers. Before they began the process which they are pleased to call "laicization" (an uncouth word, and one against which the faithful laity of France may well protest, as they do), there were 50,000 children under instruction in the Christian schools of Paris; now there are 60,000! A noble effort has been made, and all classes have combined, to raise a sum of ten million francs, to supply Christian schools to those who desire a religious education for their children; 8,000,000 have been

---

* Half a million is spent annually on the fourneaux alimentaires, or bake houses, which supply food for the children who attend the Government schools. See note at the end of the chapter.

subscribed, 2,000,000 borrowed. One hundred and twenty-eight Christian schools had been laicized or un-Christianized, and their place had to be supplied. Sites had to be found and secured, and schools built, or houses purchased and adapted. It was an enormous undertaking, and one that pressed severely upon those who were already heavily taxed for the support of the anti-Christian schools; and it could only be carried through by the cordial and united action of all who felt the vital importance of the crisis. This cordial and united action there has been. All classes have joined in it, from the wealthy who have given largely out of their abundance, to the working men who have given their labour for nothing, and the contractors who have refused all profit on their contracts. A worthy couple offered 6000 francs, the savings of a life of industry and economy; and when it was suggested to them to reserve a part for their own use, they refused, saying, "We have no children and cannot now hope to have any: take it, we are not too old to work." A small baker wrote to the Brother in charge of a school, "I have the honour to offer you from July 1 to October 31, 1879, as much bread as you want, at any price you choose to give. I am an old scholar of the Brothers, and I feel all the ingratitude there is in the proceedings which have been taken against you." And a butcher wrote, "I offer you 15 kilos.

of meat a week; I think you will not refuse to accept this offering, which is made with sincere good will."

Without such hearty co-operation, it would not have been possible to have accomplished in so short a time all that has been done. And as fast as the schools were ready they have been filled. The last reports state that applications for admission are made by thousands; at Saint Nicolas alone one hundred and sixty have been refused in one day.*

A poor working man came up from the country, early in the present year, with his wife and eight children, in search of employment, and settled in one of the suburbs of Paris. He was taken on at some glass works, at three francs a day. After his first day's work his wife persuaded him to go in the evening and get his children's names entered on the roll of the Brothers' school. As usual, there was not room for them; it should be said that he wanted to have five taken in at once. The Frère Directeur was touched by the sight of his evident great poverty, and said to him, "You had better go to the Government school (école communale); you will have help from the Poor Relief Office (bureau de bienfaisance); your children will have their school books provided gratis, and will be fed at the school 'cantine.' These are advantages which we

* "Compte rendu de l'Œuvre Diocésaine des Écoles Chrétiennes libres." Rapport de M. Denys Cochin, 1883.

are too poor to give you, and we do not like that you should miss them."

The man did as he was told, and entered his children's names at the Government school. But at nine o'clock the same evening, he knocked again at the door of the Christian school. "Mon Frère," he said, "you *must* take in my children. My wife says that in that other school they don't teach them to pray to God.—Can this be possible?— And she says too, that I must not come home to-night, till I have taken the children away from such a school as that. She is right, mon Frère; so do receive them." Somehow or other place was found for the five little ones, whose mother in her deep poverty gave up the worldly helps offered her, that they might be taught "to pray to God." Simple words, and few, but pregnant with a great truth, the expression of a great need, *the* great need of humanity, the need of God; a need which makes itself felt, consciously or unconsciously, in every soul of man, where it has not been wilfully smothered and crushed out (if indeed it *can* be smothered and crushed out); a need, the conviction of which drew from Victor Hugo these striking words, in a speech in the education debate of 1850:—

"Far from wishing to forbid religious instruction, it is, to my mind, more necessary to-day than it ever has been; in proportion to man's growth is his need of faith. The tendency to make this life everything is the misfortune of our times. If earthly life, material life, is made the only end and aim of man, all his miseries are aggravated by the negation in which they end ; to the load which weighs down the unfortunate, is added the insupportable burden of nothingness ; and that which by the ordinance of God is only suffering, becomes despair. . . . Hence arise deep social convulsions. I desire, with an inexpressible desire, to ameliorate the material lot of those who suffer, . . . but the first amelioration is to give them hope. . . . How do finite miseries diminish, when there is mingled with them an infinite hope !

" Let us say it out : death is a restitution. God is the end of all things, let us never forget it, and let us teach it to all ; there would be no dignity in life, life would not be worth the trouble, if death were an end of everything.

" That which alleviates suffering, sanctifies labour, makes man good, brave, wise, patient and strong, is to have before him the perpetual vision of another world, shining through the dark clouds of this life."

It is not the purpose of this little work to enter further into the religious or political aspects of this deeply interesting question. The book was undertaken, at the request of a revered friend, with the object of making English readers better acquainted than they commonly are with the great work of the Christian Brothers, and with the life and character of their venerable founder. Its object will be more than fulfilled if, in addition to this, it should be the means of kindling or deepening in the hearts of some English Christians affectionate sympathy for our brethren in France, who are so bravely fighting the battle in which we also are engaged, and of impressing upon some minds the lessons which may be learned from their experience.

It is true, the conflict has not yet closed in upon us as it has upon them; not yet—but signs are not wanting of the same anti-Christian spirit among us, the same hatred of everything which witnesses to a faith in the Unseen. It may be kept under for a time, but it is growing bolder and more encroaching year by year, and making visible advance. To those who are capable of forming a judgment it seems as if the outworks of the Church and of the Faith were being one by one occupied by the enemy. Who can say how soon a desperate attack may be made upon the citadel itself, and we may find ourselves, as the faithful in France now are, fighting a life and death battle in defence of all that is most sacred, most dear, and most precious to us?

One thing we know, viz. that peace there can never be; the mode of attack may vary, and the fiercest assaults may be made now in one part of the Christian camp, now in another, but peace we must not look for. It is our Captain's own word, "I am not come to send peace, but a sword." Would that the attacks of the common enemy might draw together, in visible as well as invisible unity, those whose cause is the same; that all who are on the side of Christ against anti-Christ, of faith against unfaith, of the Church against the world, might yet join hands, and own each other as " Christian Brothers." Then should we "be like unto them that dream"; then, however sorely the battle might rage, our heart would be "filled with laughter, and our tongue with joy"; then should it be "said among the heathen, the Lord hath done great things for them."

And if we dare not hope to see in our own day the realization of this "dream," let us the rather strive, each in the place assigned to us by Providence, to meet the evils of our times, in the spirit of the following words—words so full of charity and wisdom that in them we seem to "hear the conclusion of the whole matter." They are given here without their author's knowledge, in the full conviction that he would willingly have granted permission to do so, in the cause of truth and charity, and that he will not feel it an unjustifiable breach of confidence when he reads his own private letter as the concluding words of the little book which owes so much to him in other ways.

"*We must not be altogether surprised at that which is going on in France, in England, in Europe, to a certain extent everywhere. It is, under a somewhat new form, the eternal strife between good and evil. Nothing can heal the wounds of our time but charity and devotion; and, speaking generally, it is only the Christian religion which has, in its* divinity, sufficient resources to bring devotion into contact with the needs of suffering humanity.... At the present time there is a great deal of envy and hatred, because there is a great deal of suffering; and suffering is always an evil counsellor. But there is also a great deal of misunderstanding, a great deal of prejudice, a great deal of ignorance. We must each of us, in our own sphere, endeavour to dispel the latter, and to soothe the former. If we can win but one soul to a healthier and truer view of things, our time and pains will not be thrown away."

Note to page 273.

THE difference in the cost of the secular schools and those taught by members of religious orders is immense. It is evident that men and women with families cannot live as cheaply as those who have none; neither can they, nor would they, be content with the narrow cell and barely necessary furniture which is all that is provided for a Christian Brother or a Sister of Charity. Moreover, a teacher of whatever kind may fall sick, or be in other ways incapacitated, and his or her place may have to be supplied. In the case of a religious Order this is no expense; a Brother or a Sister steps at once into the vacant place, and all goes on as usual. In the case of lay teachers a substitute has to be found and paid for, and the rate of payment is far higher than what is allowed for members of religious Communities.

In the town of Lille, where the change was made some years earlier than at Paris, the boys' schools were, ten years ago, taught by 75 Christian Brothers, for each of whom a sum of 800 francs was allowed, making altogether 60,000 francs a year. This sum covered all the expenses.

Now, instead of 75 Brothers, there are 65 schoolmasters, who are assisted by sundry professors at very high salaries, and for whose recreation a club is provided. The whole expense may be reckoned under the following heads :—

	Francs.
Salaries of masters and assistants	113,775
,, professors for the boys	18,800
,, ,, for adults	10,000
,, drawing masters for boys	3,000
,, ,, ,, for adults	4,500
Maintenance of fabrics and club	8,000
	158,075f.

or an addition of 98,000 francs to the annual cost of the boys' schools alone, in one provincial town.

Bearing these facts in mind, it is not surprising to learn that the charge for primary instruction upon the public funds of the city of Paris, which in 1876, before the laicizing had begun, was nine and a half millions of francs, had in 1882 risen to twenty-three millions, and that the Budget for primary instruction for the country at large, exclusive of Paris, has advanced in even larger proportion.

The estimates which passed the Chambers, under the head of "Service de l'Instruction publique," amounted in 1878 to 53,470,714 francs; those for 1883 were 133,817,451. Under this head many charges are included which have nothing to do with primary instruction; those strictly belonging to our subject are three :—

1. Expenses of primary instruction, viz. salaries, school buildings, *encouragements* (*e.g.* food provided for the children, at a cost of 500,000 francs, and other inducements to attend the Government schools).
2. Primary instruction of adults.
3. Inspection of primary schools.

Comparing the estimates for these three heads in 1878

with those for 1883, we find the following results (the figures are taken from the "Journal officiel de la République Française"):—

	1878.	1883.
1.	20,370,200	78,620,200
2.	4,739,916	4,615,116
3.	1,889,297	2,265,297
	26,999,413 frs.	85,500,613 frs.

It may be urged that money is well bestowed on the improvement of education, and that all should be ready to bear without complaint their share of the increased taxation which it entails. But it has been shown that the increased expense has *not* improved the education; on the contrary, putting religion entirely out of the question, the less costly system, judged by results, has been proved, by tests which cannot be gainsaid, to be the best; and no more convincing proof could be given of the strong feeling which exists on the subject than the fact that such large sums should have been raised for the support of Christian schools, by voluntary contributions from those who are already so heavily rated for the maintenance of schools which they repudiate, and a system of education opposed to all that they most desire for their children.

It is true that the religious aspect of the question is that which principally influences them, probably no other motive would be sufficient for such a sacrifice, but the hardship of their case is surely much aggravated by the fact, that from a purely secular point of view the education for which they are forced to pay so dear, whether they use it or not, is inferior to what they can obtain in Christian schools. Well may such a state of things call forth indignant protests, such as that of M. Keller, who, in an eloquent speech delivered at a meeting of the Diocesan Society for Promoting Christian Education in Paris, speaking particularly of that city, exclaims, "The situation as at present is intolerable. Yes, financially it is intolerable that the inhabitants of Paris, masters and workmen, rich and poor, should have to pay double the former amount of duty on their labour, on their savings, on their food, for a system of teaching which they reject, and which runs counter to their most cherished sentiments, and that, after paying twenty-three millions for the lay schools, they should be obliged to open at their own cost free Christian schools for their children."

THE END.

www.ingramcontent.com/pod-product-compliance
Lightning Source LLC
Chambersburg PA
CBHW031330230426
43670CB00006B/301